The Spiritual Kingdom

By

Jonathan Gilchrist

Published by
TheWisdomCourse.com

The Spiritual Kingdom
by Jonathan Gilchrist

Published By

The Wisdom Course

www.TheWisdomCourse.com

Published in the United States
by TheWisdomCourse.com

Library of Congress Cataloging in Publication Data:

ISBN-10: 0615829481
ISBN-13: 9780615829487
Library of Congress Control Number: 2013910906
CreateSpace Independent Publishing Platform
North Charleston, South Carolina

Printed by CreateSpace, a d/b/a of
On-Demand Publishing LLC

Dedication:

*This book is dedicated to my mother
whose love drove her to teach me
the way to the Kingdome when
I was a child.*

CONTENTS

The Spiritual Kingdom

A Spiritual Guide to Christian Growth

By

Jonathan Gilchrist

Published by
TheWisdomCourse
Houston, Texas

INTRODUCTION

Since she was a young girl, Lemuel had always been a watcher. She watched birth and death dance between the seasons of life on the farm. She watched the young grow old, marry and bear children of their own. She watched how differently people responded to God's unexpected and sometimes unexplainable interventions in their lives.

But most of all, she loved to watch God paint almost imperceptible new details on the face of the forest, fields and friends as each year passed. No two days were ever alike.

Her hands shook as she carefully placed Esron's lunch on the old wooden tray. She slowly carried the lunch from the farmhouse out to the barn where he was working.

The farm had been her home since she was born in the old white farmhouse so long ago. Eighty years of summers had bent her back and slowed her gait to a shuffle. Years of memories flowed through her mind as she crossed the farmyard. A smile lifted the lines on her face as she remembered how her own three boys had once turned the farmyard into fierce battle-fields littered with the sound of toy gunfire, laughter and endless disagreements over who was really dead.

Lemuel began every day the same way—reading quietly from her old, worn Bible. She called it her periscope into the world—her way of seeing above the obvious, the necessary or the urgent into God's spiritual kingdom.

Lemuel sat and talked to God like an old friend. Sometimes she'd just sit there in her mother's old rocker and listen, nodding her head in silence.

"How are you feeling today?" Esron asked, interrupting her thoughts.

"I'm okay," she answered softly, brushing the dust from his shoulder.

This was a day of transition for Lemuel and Esron. Only yesterday they had heard the doctor say, "Lemuel, this will be your last summer on the farm. You have cancer and it's beginning to grow." Her lease on this body was about to expire and her spirit was about to go home.

"If there is anything you want to do, you better plan to do it now," the doctor added.

Looking death in the face made Lemuel even more aware of the life around her. Even ordinary things seemed more important than they did yesterday.

She called her son in the city and arranged for David, her ten-year-old grandson, to come to the farm for the summer. She began to pray each morning that God would show her how to teach this ten-year-old whirlwind of noise and curiosity the secret path she had learned in her eighty years on the farm.

This was her last chance. She already knew the summer would go by far too quickly for her.

The doctor's words seemed to echo back and forth in her mind.

"If there is anything you want to do, you'd better do it now."

CHAPTER ONE

THE INVISIBLE KINGDOM

---

*"There is no cry, no sound
no word in all the universe that can
be heard until someone listens."*
Unknown

"**A**re we there yet?" David asked. The long drive from the city to Granma's house seemed to take forever. The summer ahead would surprise him with days of discovery and adventure. His life was about to change forever.

Finally, his dad pulled into the long driveway to the old farmhouse. When David looked out the car window, he thought he'd been transported to another planet! Everything looked different from the city where he lived. There were no apartments, no corner store, no noisy traffic, and no people. All he could see was grass, trees, and cows.

"What's that smell?" David said. "Who died!?"

"That's the smell of the animals in the barn," his father answered. "You'll get used to it."

"I hope not!" he laughed.

Luke, Grandpa Esron's golden retriever, came running up to the car to meet David. They ran off together while David's parents helped Lemuel and Esron take David's things into the house. David's mom brought a few toys and games from the city to help him adjust to his new summer home.

David found a stick and threw it for Luke to fetch and bring back.

"Get it Luke!" he yelled.

But Luke seemed to think *he* should make the rules of the game. He decided to keep the stick instead of bringing it back. Luke and David negotiated the rules of the stick game until Lemuel called David in for dinner.

For dinner, Lemuel made mashed potatoes, fresh corn from the garden, and a big juicy steak, with peach cobbler for dessert. Dessert was David's favorite.

"This is better than a restaurant," David said.
His mother frowned. "What's wrong with my cooking?" she joked.

After dinner Esron gathered all of the leftovers and put them in a bowl for Luke. David volunteered to take Luke's dinner to him. But when he went out to the front porch, Luke wasn't there.

David was disappointed. He wanted to see Luke enjoy his meal.

"Where's Luke?" he asked Esron. "He's not here."

"I'll call him for you," Esron said. He reached in his pocket and pulled out a small silver whistle about three inches long. He blew into the whistle but no sound came out.

"It's broken," David said.

"It's not broken. That's the way it sounds," Esron answered.

Lemuel walked out to the porch as they were talking and said, "Where's Luke?"

"Grandpa tried to call him with that whistle, but I think it's broken," David said. "Nothing came out when he blew on it."

"It's a silent whistle," Lemuel said.

"A silent whistle! What good is a silent whistle?" David asked.

"It sounds silent to you, but Luke can hear it," Esron explained. "Dogs can hear higher pitched sounds than you can hear."

"It makes a sound that only a dog can hear?" David asked. "That's confusing."

"There are all kinds of sounds around you that you can't hear," Lemuel explained.

"If you can't hear it, how do you know Luke can hear it?" David asked.

"Good question," Lemuel answered. "You can't hear the dog whistle because the sound waves are too high for the human ear. Luke can hear them because his ears were made to hear that higher frequency."

"It's like radio signals," she explained. "They are all around you in the air, but you can't hear them until you tune the radio's receiver to the right frequency."

"Are there things I can't see too?" David asked as he thought about the silent whistle.

"Yes, that's right," Lemuel answered. "Just like you can't hear everything around you, your eyes only see a small part of the light waves around you. Our senses only pick up a tiny amount of the signals that surround us. Most of what surrounds us we never see or hear."

"It's like that with everything God has made," Lemuel explained. "I call it the Spiritual Kingdom. There is a world all around us that we can't see, hear or touch, but which is just as real as everything else we know."

"But if I can't see, hear or touch it, how do I know it's real?" David asked.

"What's your favorite television station?" Lemuel asked.

"Nickelodeon," David answered.

"Well, how do you know Nickelodeon exists?" she asked.

"How do I know Nickelodeon exists? I watch it every day!" David exclaimed.

"Well, where is it?" Lemuel asked. "Show it to me."

"It's on TV, and you don't have one!" David answered. "I can't show it to you without a TV."

"Yes. That's exactly the way it is with the spiritual kingdom," Lemuel explained. "There is a world around you that you will never see unless you tune in to the right channel. The only difference is that to see and hear God's spiritual kingdom, you need to tune your heart to the right frequency instead of the TV."

"I don't get it," David said.

"What happens to Nickelodeon if I pull the plug out of the wall while you are watching?" Lemuel asked.

"It goes dead," David answered.

"It's like that. We are unplugged from God on the inside and we need to get plugged in so we can see and hear what he has to show us in the spiritual kingdom," she explained.

Esron blew on the dog whistle one more time and Luke came bounding up onto the porch.

"I guess he can hear the silent whistle," David observed.

"Yes, he did," Lemuel said. "And just like Luke, you can hear and see things other people never see if you get plugged into the spiritual kingdom and tune your heart to listen."

"How do I get plugged in like you said?" David asked.

"If you ask Him, God will give you an inner voice – like that TV. tuner that we call His Spirit to show you the spiritual kingdom," Lemuel explained.

"Then, when He blows His silent whistle, you will hear it just like Luke does," she concluded.

"You'll have to show me how that works grandma," David said as he ran off to play with Luke until bedtime.

APPLYING THE LESSON

At first it seems like a contradiction: a whistle that doesn't produce any sound? The apparent contradiction is only solved when we learn about how the dog whistle actually works.

In much the same way, we live in a spiritual world that we can't see or understand until we learn how it actually works. We don't hear its message or see how its principles work until we first see the secret kingdom where spiritual reality exists.

Jesus noticed this same problem when the people of Israel just couldn't understand what he was talking about when he described the spiritual kingdom.

"You will be ever hearing but never understanding; You will be ever seeing but never perceiving. For this people's hearts are calloused."
Matthew 13:14

Jesus spoke of spiritual reality but, like the dog whistle, most people just couldn't hear it. He often said, "He who has ears to hear, let him hear." (Mark 4:9). He realized that most of his listeners did not have their hearts tuned to the right frequency. As a result, they weren't getting the spiritual message he was speaking. Like radio waves in the air, you don't hear the message unless you tune to the correct frequency.

Jesus' words were 'spirit and life,' but to people whose lives were tuned to the wrong channel, they only heard nice stories and parables. They couldn't see past the natural world to hear the spiritual message.

Late one night Nicodemus, a famous teacher of the law and a member of the Jewish senate, came to Jesus privately to discuss what he was teaching. Jesus told him that the spiritual life was like the wind—you couldn't hear it or pin it down, but you know it is real. Nicodemus still couldn't understand the spiritual meaning of what Jesus was telling him.

Surprised that this famous rabbi did not understand spiritual reality, Jesus said, "I have spoken to you of earthly things and you do not believe. How then will you believe if I speak to you of heavenly things?" (John 3:12).

Because Nicodemus did not have his life tuned to hear spiritual truth, he could not understand what Jesus meant. Jesus told Nicodemus he must connect to his inner spiritual self and there find the spiritual reality of the kingdom. "No one can see the kingdom of God unless he is born again," Jesus said. (John 3:3).

Paul learned of this spiritual kingdom when he dramatically encountered God on the road to Damascus, stating:

> *"For who among men knows the thoughts of a man except the man's spirit within him? In the same way no one knows the thoughts of God except the Spirit of God.*
>
> *"We have not received the spirit of the world but the Spirit who is from God, that we may understand what God has freely given us. This is what we speak, not in words taught us by human wisdom but in words taught by the Spirit, expressing spiritual truth in spiritual words.*
>
> *"The man without the spirit does not accept the things that come from the Spirit of God, for they are foolishness to him, and he cannot understand them, because they are spiritually discerned."*
>
> I Corinthians 2:11, 12.

Because God is spiritual, He speaks to us as spiritual beings. If we have never become spiritually alive, we cannot hear what He is saying. He speaks of spiritual reality to those who have entered the spiritual kingdom; but like Luke responding to the dog whistle, we must have "ears to hear."

In this book we will explore a kingdom that is just as real as the physical world in which you live but which lies beyond the realm of the five senses—the place where eternity exists. It is where we get in touch with the eternal, lasting part of who we are as well.

It is in this spiritual place that we discover the source of life, its true meaning and its final destination. It is here in the spiritual kingdom that man touches the reality of God and discovers what he is made of.

As we follow Lemuel and David through this book, listen for the inner spiritual voice of God. He will speak to the spiritual part of who you are—below the surface of your five senses.

When you hear the soft whisper of the Spirit's voice, tune in a little closer and listen. Cultivate the skill of listening to what God is saying to you and your hearing will improve.

When you begin to follow the sound of God's voice, you begin your journey into the spiritual kingdom, a journey inward that draws you closer to God the farther you walk. There you will learn life's ultimate intention: a life lived with God as your friend in a reality that you couldn't even see before you started the spiritual journey of life.

SPIRITUAL EXERCISE:

> *"The more faithfully you listen to the voice within you, the better you will hear the sounding outside. And only those who listen can speak."*
> Dag Hammerskjold, *Markings*

Paul was not just a writer, teacher and church planter; he was a personal trainer—spiritually. He always took a small group of young men with him to watch and listen to everything he did. He taught them both the practical skills of ministry and the spiritual reality of the kingdom.

This is what Lemuel did with David during his summer at the farm. She used ordinary things they encountered each day to teach David spiritual principles he could use for the rest of his life. She was a tour guide to David, a personal spiritual trainer, explaining the deeper significance of ordinary events so that David could learn the secrets of the Spiritual Kingdom.

As a trainer, Paul also required his students to take responsibility and to practice what he taught them. For example, he would often send his letters to the churches with one of his students. He gave them the job of teaching the message just as if he had been there himself. He didn't just tell them what to do; he had them actually practice what he taught them.

Each chapter in this book will include practical spiritual exercises to help you internalize the lesson Lemuel teaches David.

In a letter he wrote to one of the students he was training (Timothy), Paul says, "train yourself to be Godly . . . be diligent in these matters; give yourself to them, so that everyone may see your progress."

(I Timothy 4:7, 15).

Just as going to the gym and working out makes the muscles grow stronger, so spiritual exercises strengthen your spiritual life.

Lemuel showed David that there was an entire world around him that he couldn't perceive with his five senses.

We live in this world without thinking about it. The more we learn to see this spiritual world, the more we grow spiritually.

Spiritual Exercise, Part I: In the space below think of five things that you know exist but which cannot be verified by any of our five natural senses. For example, Lemuel talked about the sound of the dog whistle, radio waves and television signals. You might also consider things like love, faith, hope, etc.

Five elements of reality that I cannot touch, taste, smell, hear or see:

1. _____

2. _____

3. _____

4. _____

5. _____

Lemuel taught David how God gives to each person an ability to perceive—to hear—spiritual things. By doing the spiritual exercises in this book you can begin to translate this spiritual reality into the substance of who you are.

Spiritual Exercise, Part II: To begin this process, spend five minutes each day for the next week in complete, uninterrupted silence. Find a place with no distractions—no radio, no TV, no children. At first it will be hard to keep your mind from interrupting the silence with self-talk, but focus and find your quiet heart.

When you find that quiet inner place in your own heart, tell God that you have come to find the way of His Spirit and to learn how to hear the sound of His voice. This is an exercise. Do it each day.

> *"We need to find God, and he cannot be found in noise and restlessness. God is the friend of silence. The more we receive in silent prayer, the more we can give in our active lives."*
> Mother Teresa, *Something Beautiful for God*

> *"It is not my business to think about myself. My business is to think about God. It is for God to think about me."*
> Simone Weil

CHAPTER TWO

GRASPING THE SPIRITUAL

---

*"For this is the truth we must live,
that everything is and we just in it."*
Dag Hammarskjold

One sunny June day, Lemuel packed a picnic lunch for David. She made fried chicken, homemade potato salad and his favorite dessert – pecan pie. They walked down to the picnic spot near the duck pond to enjoy their mid-day adventure.

It was a perfect day. They soaked in the warm sun and watched the clouds paint a perfect picture in the reflection of the pond's still waters. They challenged each other to see who could find the most animal shapes in clouds. Suddenly, a gust of wind rolled across the pond, and the reflection of the sky disappeared under a thousand silver ripples.

David watched for a moment and then asked, "Grandma, how does the wind erase the picture of the clouds from the water?"

Lemuel thought for a moment and said, "Next time the breeze comes, run down to the pond and catch a handful of it so we can see what it is made of."

David didn't think that was a very good answer, but he did it anyway just to see what would happen. He jumped into the air near the pond, grasping at the air trying to get a handful to bring back to Lemuel. But each time he opened his hand, it was empty!

"There's nothing there, Grandma!" he exclaimed.

"Come sit here and eat your lunch. I'll explain it to you," Lemuel said calmly.

"When you open your hand, you say there is nothing there. But you see the waves on the water and you hear the wind blow through the leaves in the tree. You can feel it on your skin. How can you say there is nothing there?" She asked.

"Because when I opened my hand it was empty!" David answered.

"Many people feel that way about God," Lemuel said. "They try to prove He's real but they can't get a hold of him just like you couldn't catch the wind," she explained.

"When Nicodemus came to Jesus that night, he was asking the same question. He wanted to find God. Jesus explained to him that finding God was like catching the wind. But when you tried, you couldn't catch it, could you?" Lemuel asked.

"My hand was empty," David replied.

Lemuel continued, "Jesus said, 'the wind blows wherever it wants to, you hear its sound, but you cannot tell where it comes from or where it is going.' That's the way it is when you find God. It's like catching the wind."

"But I can't catch the wind," David explained.

"You are right," Lemuel answered. "But you can let it catch you! You can't grab the wind and take control of it. But you see it move the water, you hear it blow the leaves and you feel it against your skin. You know it's real. You just can't catch it."

"Do you remember reading in school about Columbus' first voyage to America?" she asked.

David nodded.

"One day, far out in the Atlantic Ocean the wind suddenly stopped blowing and Columbus' boats drifted for weeks. With no wind, the boats couldn't move toward land. The crew was running out of food and getting frustrated. Then, early one morning, the wind began to blow again. Columbus put up his sails and made it the rest of the way to America. It's like that in your spiritual life too. Without the wind of God in your sails, you won't go anywhere," she concluded.

"I don't get it," David said. "How is finding God like trying to catch the wind?"

"In the Bible, God explains that finding Him is like finding the wind for your sails. God doesn't live in a physical body like you do. So he uses something you are familiar with, the wind, to explain what He is like."

"He said, 'the wind blows wherever it wants to. You hear its sound, but you cannot tell where it comes from or where it is going. So it is with everyone born of the Spirit,'" she added. [John 3:8]

Lemuel was speaking softly and David could tell this was important to her.

"In the ancient language of the Bible, the word for wind and the word for God's spirit are exactly the same word. Jesus used this word play to explain to Nicodemus what it is like to find God," she said.

"Here. Do this," Lemuel said. "Put your hand in front of your mouth and see what comes out when you talk."

"I feel little puffs of wind against my hand," David said.

"That's right! You create a wind that carries your words to others even though you stay right where you are after you say the words," Lemuel said.

"The words are on their own now!" David said with a chuckle.

"Yes, that's it," Lemuel replied with a smile. "The wind has the power and life of its own once you release it."

"At the beginning of the Bible, it says God spoke the things we see around us into existence just like you spoke those words. Everything we see and feel is a result of what He created a long time ago. To God, this world is like the wind you felt on your hand as you spoke those words. It came out from Him but now it's on its own."

"Jesus used this picture of the wind to explain how it feels when God comes near. When He comes, you will feel His presences inside of you just like you feel the gentle touch of the wind on your hand. You will feel something move inside of you like you saw the ripples on the pond when the wind came."

"Then you know that God wants to move your heart just like the wind moved Columbus' boats when they were stuck in the middle of the ocean. All you have to do is open up the sails of your heart and let the wind take you where you need to go," she added.

"Listen for the wind. Be open to it. Let it push you in the right direction."

"What we learned today, David, is that, although you can never catch the wind, you can let it catch you. If you follow the wind, you will always end up where God wants you to be," she said.

The sat there quietly for a long time as David thought about what Lemuel had said and ate his pecan pie.

APPLYING THE LESSON

Lemuel had discovered that the secret of a happy life was to live in the presence of God—where she could always feel the breeze. When Jesus taught about the kingdom of God, He used a play on words that we don't see in the English translation; He used exactly the same word for the Spirit, by which we are 'born' a second time as He did to describe the wind. (The Greek word *pneuma*, which means, "wind" or "breath," and which is also translated as "spirit" in the New Testament.)

In the original language in which it was written, you see the words for wind and breath used over and over again to describe the power and presence of God. A strong east wind blew to part the Red Sea so that the people of Israel could walk across on dry ground. A mighty rushing wind filled the upper room near the temple where the disciples first experienced the presence of the Holy Spirit on Pentecost. In the book of

Genesis, the Hebrew word for the life-giving breath that God breathed into Adam means a gust of wind.

There's an interesting story of God's 'breath' in Ezekiel's vision of the Valley of Dry Bones. God takes Ezekiel to a hill overlooking a valley. The ground is covered with dry human bones. He tells Ezekiel to prophesy that God will "make *breath* enter you, and you will come to life." Ezekiel did what he was told to do. Suddenly he heard the bones begin to rattle and come together. He saw them miraculously become covered with muscle and flesh - they looked alive, but they were still just dead corpses with no life in them.

Then God said to Ezekiel, "prophesy to the *breath*." So Ezekiel invokes the power of the wind, and "breath entered them, they came to life and lived."

The Bible explains that this is an illustration of what would happen in the future when He would put His Spirit in His children—they would come alive in a new way.

I think some Christians today have not experience everything that this story illustrates. They look renewed on the outside, like the corpses in the desert, but they have not yet been filled with the inner wind of life that God's Spirit brings. Until the living presence of God enters our lives, we are still spiritually dead—even if we look like we are put together right. That is the spiritual message of Ezekiel's story.

The presence of God often comes as a soft, almost imperceptible wind. It becomes within us a source of new life that lifts us above the boundaries of the physical senses into the eternal, spiritual kingdom.

Jesus told us that we must take on the character of the wind: "The wind blows wherever it pleases.

You hear its sound, but you cannot tell where it comes from or where it is going. So it is with everyone born of the Spirit." John 3:8

Once the Spirit dwells within, a new spiritual, un-catchable, unpredictable, fluid nature takes over our heart that transcends the physical world—it is spiritual life.

To reach its goal, a ship must open its sails and leave its home port. It has to be disconnected from the comfort of the dock and set free to follow the ocean tides. The breeze of God's Spirit will fill the sails of our hearts if they are open and guide us to His spiritual kingdom.

SPIRITUAL EXERCISE

Three hundred years ago, a young woman named Jeanne-Marie Guyon started searching for God. She was hungry on the inside.

She read every book of theology she could get her hands on, studied the Bible intensely, and prayed as hard as she could—yet, it seemed like God was always just beyond her reach.

Then, one day, a Franciscan monk, who had just re-turned from spending five years in solitude with God, visited her small town in France. Her father arranged for her to meet the monk because of her great hunger to find God.

The monk's message to Jeanne-Marie was similar to what Lemuel told David by the pond.

After listening to all she had done in her search for God and seeing her frustration, the monk said to her, *"It is, Madame, because you seek without what can only be found within.   Accustom yourself to seek God in your heart and you will find Him there."*

Jesus said the same thing to the religious leaders of Israel: "The kingdom of God does not come with your careful observation, nor will people say, 'Here it is,' or 'There it is,' because the kingdom of God is within you." (Luke 17:20, 21.)

She describes her feeling when she heard those words, recounting, "They were to me like the stroke of a dart, which penetrated through my heart. I felt a very deep wound, a wound so delightful that I desired not to be cured. These words brought into my heart what I had been seeking so many years. Rather they discovered to me what was there, and which I had not enjoyed for want of knowing it." (*Autobiography of Madam Guyon*).

Spiritual Exercise, Part I: Prayer: In the last chapter, we be began to practice finding a place of silence in our own hearts where the kingdom of God can be seen and heard. Today, we will take that exercise one step further.

Find a place away from all noise and distraction; quiet the voice of your mind until you can hear the quiet breeze of the Spirit's voice inside of you.

Like standing outside in a gentle breeze, you can't tell exactly where it is coming from or where it is going. Just enjoy the feeling of the wind. This is not about doing something; this exercise is about learning to feel and to listen. It is practice in letting God say what He wants, how He wants, when He wants.

Don't try to analyze what you feel or you may end up like David near the pond when he tried to catch the wind—his hands came up empty.

Jesus said, "If any man is thirsty, let him come and drink." (John 7:37). And to the woman from Samaria, he said, "If you knew the gift of God and who it is that is asks you for a drink, you would have asked Him and He would have given you living water." (John 4:10). Because this water is spiritual, it flows in your heart.

When you sense the breeze of God's presence, just tell him you are thirsty for His living water and ask Him for a drink. It's something He wants to give you. Practice and learn what the Spirit feels like inside of you. This exercise will help you learn to recognize God's voice better even when it is soft and hard to hear. You can come back to the stream and drink any time you want.

Spiritual Exercise, Part II: Meditation: Jesus taught us that the Spirit of God operates inside of us like the wind upon the earth. In the spaces below list five attributes of the wind that are similar to the way God moves and works.

1. _____

2. _____

3. _____

4. _____

5. _____

CHAPTER THREE

BUILD THE FIRE

"It is I who created the blacksmith
who fans the coals into flame
and forges a weapon fit for its work."
Isaiah 54:16

On the north side of Lemuel and Esron's farm lay eighty acres of dense forest. Otter Creek ran along the far side of the forest and beyond that was a large national forest.

Having David at the farm brought back years of memories for Lemuel and Esron. They remembered the years when David's father had grown up there as a boy. So, one weekend they decided to pull the old tent and camp-stove out of the storage shed and take David to the national forest for an overnight camping trip.

David was so excited that all week long he couldn't sit still. He and Lemuel made a list of everything they would need to take on the big adventure—food, a flashlight, matches, the hatchet, and on and on the list went.

Lemuel baked cookies and snacks to take along while Esron got all of the camping gear cleaned and ready to go. They even found a couple of old canvas sleeping bags in the garage and aired them out on the clothesline.

"This week is going so slow it feels like waiting for Christmas," David said.

On Friday afternoon when the chores were done, they all piled into Esron's pickup truck and drove to the edge of the north pasture near the forest. Each person carried part of the gear as they headed off into the forest for their adventure.

They walked so far, David was sure they were lost.

"It seems dark and quiet in here," David noted.

Finally, they reached a small clearing in the woods just north of Otter Creek. "This is a good place to set up camp," Esron said. It's sunny here and we're close to the water."

David and Esron set up the tent while Lemuel unpacked the food and supplies. David wandered into the forest to explore but soon was back at the tent.

"What's to eat, Grandma," he said. "I'm hungry from all that work."

"If you want me to cook, you're going to have to build a fire," Lemuel answered. She only had to say that once!

David quickly gathered a few leaves to get the fire started. He got three big armloads of dead branches and broke them up for firewood.

He built a neat pile of firewood and lit the leaves with a match. They burned up quickly went out just as fast. "The fire won't start," David complained.

"You need to get some smaller braches for kindling and fan the flames until the larger branches catch fire," Esron explained. He helped David get some dry kindling and start the fire.

David enjoyed playing in the fire. He gathered branches and put them on the fire all evening long. After a couple of hours, he was getting tired of trying to find more wood for the fire because his branches kept burning up.

"Grandma, where does the wood go when it gets burned up by the fire?" he asked.

Lemuel had to think a minute about that one. "Well, David," she replied, "did you notice how the wood slowly disappears as it is burned by the flames? What you see is the mystery of the wood and the fire becoming one. The heat from the fire excites the molecules in the wood and as the molecules vibrate from the heat, the structure of the wood changes. It changes from solid wood to heat, vapor and flame—then you don't see it any more."

"Yeah, but the fire keeps going out if I don't put more wood on it," David said. "I'm tired of getting more wood all the time."

"The fire depends on the wood to make the heat and flame that cooks the food," Lemuel explained. "Without wood, the fire goes out; and without the fire, the wood produces no heat. They need each other."

Then she added, "God says we all have to fan the gifts that He puts in our hearts into flame, just like you did when you got the fire started."

"What does that mean?" David asked.

"Well," Lemuel replied, "just like you needed wood to start the fire, God put in each of us the potential for spiritual life—like the wood sitting in the forest waiting for you to come get it today. He is like the flame on the wood—He turns hearts that are like old dead limbs into warm burning fires."

"The Bible uses the picture of fire to describe what it is like when God comes to live inside of us. Remember the story of how the disciples where hiding in Jerusalem after He died? Jesus told them to wait there for God to come visit them. They didn't know what to expect, but they did what He said because they knew Him. They waited for ten days."

"Suddenly, one day, they heard a wind blow through the room and they saw little flames like fire come to each person. The Bibles says that is when God filled them with His sprit. That was God's way of painting a picture for us so we can see what it is like when He fills us with His spirit."

"But, I don't get how that's like the wood and the fire that we used to cook supper," David said.

"It's just like what you saw when the fire make the wood disappear," Lemuel answered. "God says His spirit will change our lives just like the fire changed the wood."

"But, it burned it all up!" David exclaimed.

"It's like that in our hearts too," Lemuel answered. "God's spirit in us is like a fire that changes our hearts until the we get turned into something that looks like Him instead of who we used to be. Like the fire change the wood into heat, flame and energy, God turns us into a spiritual person like He is."

"But what happens to me if I get burnt up by God?" David asked.

"Just like the wood on the fire, you are still here but you are different than you were before," Lemuel explained. "You have been joined to the flame like the wood and the fire so that people can't tell you apart anymore."

"God changes you from a natural person like the branch of wood, into a spiritual person like the fire and the flame. Now, you are part of the spiritual kingdoms."

APPLYING THE LESSON

Have you ever tried to explain Einstein's theory of relativity to someone? It's hard to explain how matter and energy are interchangeable—essentially the same stuff existing in different forms. Because we see, feel and touch the physical all day long, it seems difficult to understand that what we see can be transformed into invisible energy, and that electrons and protons could be changed back into mater. But it's true! Just because it is hard to get our head around doesn't mean it isn't a scientific fact.

We have the same difficulty trying to explain that the essential element of who we are as a person is spiritual, not the physical person that we see and touch. But once we grasp that fact, we can begin to understand the truth that God is also a spirit and that it is possible for these two spirits to be joined together as one.

In science, the fact that reality lies beyond what we see can be hard to understand. The spiritual kingdom is exactly the same—it's real but the fact that it exists beyond our sight makes it a challenge to comprehend.

The apostle Paul tried to explain this when he said, "So we fix our eyes not on what is seen, but on what is unseen. For what is seen is temporary, but what is unseen is eternal." (2 Corinthians 4:18)

The Bible uses the analogy of death followed by a new birth to illustrate the total change that occurs when a human spirit meets God's spirit and is transformed like the wood into the flame. Once a life surrenders to the flame, it is forever altered. The spiritual life—like the flame replacing the original wood—now becomes the core of who we are.

Paul explains it this way: "I no longer live, but Christ lives in me. The life that I live in the body, I live by faith in the son of God, who loved me and gave Himself for me." (Galatians 2:20). Paul says that the man he used to be has been transformed into a new, spiritual person united with God's spirit, just like the flame and the wood becoming one. That means that if I yield to God's spirit, I must surrender to His right to change me from a natural, object-oriented person into a person guided and controlled by what is spiritual.

Remember that there was a process during which the fire was transforming the wood—it didn't happen in an instant. The goal is for the fire, or in this case the Spirit, to consume the old wood and transform it into fire and flame. That's what God does. He consumes the old nature and replaces it with a new spiritual nature.

Because, when the new comes—the fire and the flame—the old disappears (like the old firewood), Paul calls it a death of the old self.

Jesus' close friend, John, writes the same 'good news' in his first letter to the church: "we have passed from death to life." (I John. 3:14).

Just like the wood on David's campfire was transformed into invisible fire, vapor and energy when it was joined to the flame, so we are changed into spiritual beings when God's Spirit takes over our lives.

> *"To possess Him who cannot be understood is to renounce all that can be understood. To rest in Him who is beyond all created rest, we renounce the desire to rest in created things.*
>
> *"This is what Jesus meant when He said that anyone who would save his life will lose it, and he who would lose his life, for the sake of God, would save it."*
>
> Thomas Merton, *Thoughts in Solitude*

SPIRITUAL EXERCISE

The process of yielding to God irrevocably changes us. When you choose to yield to God, you must accept that a significant transformation is about to occur. Watchman Nee uses the illustration of a dinner roll to describe the effect on our lives of yielding to the power of God. Once the roll is broken, it can never be put back together again—it has been permanently changed.

Two characteristics of firewood make it hard to burn: hardness or rottenness. For us, hardness represents those places in our lives where we have closed the door to God in order to hang on to the person we used to be. Rottenness, on the other hand, represents those places in our lives where we have failed to maintain boundaries. As a result, the structure of our character and integrity has begun to decompose like rotting wood.

The first part of this exercise is an act of prayer and self-analysis. Take a notebook or several pieces of paper and find a quiet place where you will not be interrupted for at least an hour. If you need to, get out of the house and go to a park or a library so you can concentrate. This is an exercise in listening.

Begin with this prayer:

"God, I know that there are hard places in my heart where I have closed the door due to pain, pride or self-interest. Right now, I invite you to enter those closed rooms and to examine my inner thoughts and feelings. Here, I'm giving you the key to every room.

"Show me, through Your spirit, every place that I have not yielded to you to be transformed by the presence of Your life in me. I will listen and write down what you bring to my mind."

Now, open your eyes and write down the first thing that comes to your mind.

Don't analyze, evaluate, or consider what you feel, just write it down for now. You will analyze it later. You may feel uncertain whether your thoughts are from God or not, but that's okay. Just write down what comes to your mind and use this as an exercise—you don't have to be good at it yet.

For thirty minutes, write down whatever God brings to your mind. When you have finished, take a short break, and then come back and do the same exercise for areas of rottenness in your life—areas of pride, lust, greed, selfishness, bitterness or laziness. Let God reveal areas of weakness that you might not think about because they have become a recurring part of your everyday life. It is only after you see your weakness that you can correct it.

Spiritual Exercise, Part II: Now you are going to build a real fire. If possible, go to a state park or campground and build a fire. Otherwise, you can use a barbeque pit or grill.

When you have your fire burning, take the lists that you made in Part I of this Spiritual Exercise and begin to talk to God about each of them.

Tell Him you want to let Him be the fire that takes the hard places and rottenness out of your life and replaces them with spiritual life.

Read each item on your list that God brought to your mind. As you read, make it your choice and prayer to give each thing on your list to God to be consumed by Him. Then put that part of your list on the fire so it can be burned. As you see the fire consume you list of hard places and rotten spots in your life, yield them to God in your heart at the same time.

Choose to yield these hidden parts of your heart to God so that He can change them for you.

> *"There are but two states, or forms of life, the one is natural, and the other is God manifested in the natural; and as God and nature are both within you, so you have it in your power to live*

and work with either, but you must choose one or the other.

"A now, sir, you see the absolute necessity of the doctrine of the cross, that is, of dying to self, as the one and only way to life in God."

William Law

CHAPTER FOUR

THE BIG CHANGE

---

*"It happened that a fire broke out backstage
in a theater. A clown came out to inform
the public about it. They thought it was a
joke and applauded. He repeated it; people
laughed even more. This is the way I think
the world will end – with general giggling
by all who think it is a joke."*
Soren Kierkegaard, *Either Or*

After breakfast on Monday morning, Lemuel decided to take David fishing in the big stock pond near the far side of the east pasture. As they walked to the pasture, Lemuel told David how her grandfather had stocked the pond with fish when she was a little girl. David brought one of Esron's old fishing poles and a tin can of fresh worms he had dug at the edge of the garden that morning.

At the west end of the pond stood an old elm tree with a rope on one limb to swing out into the water. Here three generations of children had spent their summers swimming and waging water wars.

David had never gone fishing before. He was excited about catching lunch for Lemuel and Esron. David picked a spot on the side of the pond, just past the swimming area, where he was sure the big fish would be waiting for him. He took the first worm from the can and tried to get it on the hook—it was not cooperating. Finally, he got the hook through the worm a couple of times and dropped his line into the edge of the water.

"You might do a little better if you cast your bait just a little farther out," Lemuel suggested. "I think your worm is sitting on the bottom of the lake hiding from the fish."

"Okay," David said, as he reeled in his line. "Here it goes!" he said as he gave the line a powerful cast, only to find that the worm was still caught on a stick lying on the ground behind him.

"Would you like me to show you how to cast it?" Lemuel asked.

David handed her the pole, and she showed him how to hold the pole and cast the bait out into the pond.

"Now I can do it," David said as he took the pole from Lemuel. He cast the line about five feet out into the water and said, "See, I've got it now."

Just then his bobber disappeared under the water and popped right back up again. David jerked the line as hard as he could, nearly catching Lemuel with the hook as it flew by. The hook was empty.

"Where'd my worm go?" David asked. "How did the fish get my worm without getting caught?"

"If you bait your hook so that the fish can eat the bait without getting hooked it will. You will lose your worm but not catch any fish," she answered. "There is a lot to learn about how to be a good fisherman, just as there is a lot to learn about how to be a good person,"

"I'm already a good person," David said.

"You are a good person," she agreed. "But as you grow older, being a good person will mean much more than it means today. There's a whole world inside you that no one else sees. It is in that world that you learn to live a good life or an ineffective life."

"Look," David interrupted. "There's a school of minnows. Maybe I should catch some to use for bait so I can catch bigger fish."

"Those aren't minnows," Lemuel answered. "They are tadpoles. They only look like minnows. Pretty soon they will be frogs."

"Frogs?" David asked. "They don't look anything like frogs. How can a minnow become a frog?"

"Come, look over here," Lemuel said as she walked down toward the muddy end of the pond. "Look down there in the water by the lily pads." "Are those minnows or tadpoles?" David asked.

"Those are tadpoles," Lemuel answered. "If you look closely, you will see that they don't have scales like the minnows and fish do. That's because, even thought the tadpoles look like little fish, God made them to become something different from what they started out as."

"Look, Grandma," David said. "There's something wrong with that one. It looks like it is hurt or something."

"No, that's what's supposed to happen," Lemuel replied. "What is happening is that the tadpole is starting to grow legs so that it can climb from the pond and live the life of a frog."

"I don't get how a tadpole can become a frog," David said. "In the water there is no air. I see the tadpole breathing through its gills just like a fish does. Won't it die if it comes out of the water?"

"If it come out of the water before God finished transforming its lungs, it would die," Lemuel answered. "God has to give it a new way of breathing, a new way of walking, and a new way of gathering food before it can live outside the water."

"I think you're pulling my leg, Grandma," David said. "There's no way these minnows can ever become frogs. You think that just because I grew up in the city I will believe anything."

"We'll see," Lemuel answered. "Let's go back to the house and fix lunch. I don't think we're going to catch any fish today. We'll come back and try again tomorrow."

Esron laughed when David told him the story of how Lemuel had tried to convince him that water-breathing tadpoles somehow could be transformed into air-breathing frogs.

"That does sound like a hard story to swallow," Esron said with a smile. "Maybe you should go back there in a few days and explore whether that story is true or not."

David liked fishing at the pond, so he and Lemuel started to go fishing every couple of days.

"Let's see how the minnows are doing," David said. "I want to see if they can walk yet," he laughed.

They walked down to the muddy end of the pond and looked down by the lily pads. David was surprised at what he saw.

"Look, Grandma," David said. "They do have legs! I thought you were kidding. How will they breath if they get out of the water?"

"God made tadpoles with the special ability to live in two different kingdoms," she answered. "They can live in the water and breathe through their gills or they can walk out onto the land and breath through their lungs."

"What happens if a tadpole decides it does not want to be a frog and just decides to stay in the water instead of walking onto the land?"

"If a tadpole doesn't come out of the water when it is supposed to, it will die in the water without ever knowing what it is like to be a frog that can jump, breath and live on the beach near the pond. It's sort of like the way God made us."

"What do you mean, that's the way He made us?" David asked. "I can't breath under water."

"No." Lemuel answered with a laugh. "You are not going to live in the water like the frog, but God made it so that you can live in two different kingdoms; two different kinds of worlds. If you choose not to leave the first kingdom and enter the second kingdom you will end up dying there without ever experiencing the life God had planned for you. You will be like the tadpole that refused to leave the water and never learned to jump on dry land."

"Hello? Earth to Grandma!" David laughed. "That doesn't even make sense. I'm a person and I always will be. How can you say that God wants me to be something else?"

"It is hard to understand until you've been there," Lemuel agreed. "People didn't understand Jesus when he talked to them either. But we are born into a natural, physical world—like the tadpole in the water. What many people don't understand is that God plans for us to grow out of that natural world and into the Spiritual world that exists all around us like the dry land all around the pond. I call it God's spiritual kingdom."

"How is living in the spiritual kingdom any different from living here?" David asked.

"When we enter the spiritual kingdom we do still live here," Lemuel explained. "What is different is that we learn to see things differently, feel things differently, and respond to things differently when we enter the spiritual kingdom.

"When the tadpole becomes a frog, it keeps the same blood, brain, and body, but it is transformed so that it can breathe the air and experience a whole world it didn't even know existed when it lived in the water. It can still jump back into the pond and swim if it wants to, but now it knows how to experience the world outside of the water."

"I don't understand what you mean about the spiritual kingdom," David said. "I can see, hear and touch everything around me. How can there be something else that I can't see?"

"Come over here and look at this," Lemuel said. "Here's a little frog that still has a tadpole tail. It is just learning how to walk, breath and jump on the land."

"Let me catch it," David said, reaching for the polliwog. "Oh, man, it got away!" he exclaimed as it jumped away from him. "It sure knew how to get back in the water in a hurry."

"Of course it did," Lemuel replied. "That's where it has spent its entire life. Look at it swimming around with the other tadpoles that haven't gotten out of the water yet. What do you think they're talking about?"

"He's probably telling them he almost got caught!" David laughed.

"Do you think he will tell them about the things he has seen outside of the pond?" Lemuel asked. "About the trees and grass, the sun and wind; about catching flies and jumping on the dry ground?"

"If I was a frog, I would tell them to get out of the water and have some fun on the dry land."

"What if they don't believe him?" Lemuel replied. "None of them has ever seen the things he is telling them about. It must sound pretty unrealistic to a minnow to hear about all of the things that the frog has seen on the dry land."

"I'll bet they think his brain got fried in the sun," David laughed.

"Maybe they do," Lemuel answered. "But remember what you said when I told you about God's spiritual kingdom? About the whole new world of life and experience that God has planned for us to experience if we will leave the pond we were born in and follow Him into the new life He has planned for us?"

"I remember," David said. "I told you I didn't believe you because it didn't' make sense to me that there is another whole world that I don't even know exists."

"You sound just like a tadpole listening to a frog," Lemuel smiled. "By the way, who was right, the tadpole or the frog?"

"Well, the frog was right because he had actually been outside the pond and had seen what was there." David answered.

"That's exactly the way it is with finding God's spiritual kingdom. To understand what it is really like you need to talk with someone who has already been there," Lemuel explained.

"Have you been there?" David asked.

"Yes, David. When I was nine years old, my mother told me about the spiritual kingdom and showed me how to find it. I have spent the last seventy years learning as much as I could about the spiritual world that God first showed me that day."

"How did she tell you to find it?" David asked.

"It was just like the frog. All I had to do was climb out of the water and go there," Lemuel answered. "My mother told me that to find the spiritual kingdom I needed to turn my heart toward God and talk to Him about what I wanted; to tell Him that I wanted to come into the Kingdom where He was in control. I needed to learn to live in His presence like the frog learning to breath the air when it hopped out of the water. I learned to get a new kind of nutrition from the Bible and His words to me."

"Was that hard to do?"

"No, that was the easy part," Lemuel explained. "It was learning how to breath, jump and feed myself in the new kingdom that was hard to do. But nothing I ever did made me happier than spending my time with God in the new kingdom."

"Can anyone get into the spiritual kingdom that wants to?"

"Yes, they can. When Jesus came to earth to live, He said that anyone who wanted to could come and live in the spiritual kingdom."

"What do I need to do if I want to get into the spiritual kingdom?" David asked.

"It's not hard," Lemuel responded. "You just need to do what I did when I was a young girl. You need to tell God in your heart what you want and that you have decided to come into His kingdom and that you want to learn to walk with Him and be one of His spiritual children. He will help you with everything that comes after that."

"What do I say?"

"Just tell Him exactly what you want."

David sat there for a few minutes on the bank of the pond and watched the tadpoles and polliwogs swimming around the lily pads. Pretty soon one of the polliwogs climbed out of the water onto the sandy shore and took a big breath of fresh air.

"Okay," David said. "I'm going to do it." He looked out across the pond and then back at the polliwog on the beach. "God, Grandma says that You have a whole new kingdom that I don't know about yet where You treat us like your children and we learn new things from You. I want to be like this polliwog that just climbed out of the water; I want to go into Your spiritual kingdom. I know I have a lot of things to learn; so I'll need You to help me. Thanks."

"Now what do I do?" David asked.

"You give me a hug. That's what you do." Lemuel said as a happy tear ran down her cheek. "God will show you the things that you should do," she added. "We'll talk more about it while you're here this summer, but for now let's go tell Esron what you decided to do."

APPLYING THE LESSON

Is there life outside the pond? To the tadpole, the only world that is real is what exists under the surface of the water.

Is man more than a cleverly constructed pile of chemicals? Is there something in the essence of humanity that survives the eventual death of the body?

David looked into the pond and saw minnows, because he had never seen the transforming power of a frog's genetics. He just couldn't believe that a water-breathing tadpole could become an air-breathing frog.

Many people respond like David when they hear the news of God's spiritual kingdom. They are like the tadpole listening to a frog explain what life is like out of the water. It just seems unreal and impossible.

Many of the people who heard Jesus speak in person had the same reaction—it was just too much to believe because it was totally outside of their personal experience.

It is hard for a tadpole to believe it can become a frog. Yet it can, and it will. It was born with the nature of the frog within it.

In much the same way, man is made to live a spiritual life of communion with God.

Paul writes, "He chose us in Him before the creation of the world to be holy and blameless . . . to be adopted as His sons through Jesus Christ."

Ephesians 1:4, 5.

Now, just because a tadpole is created to become a frog, doesn't mean it's easy for the tadpole to believe that's what will happen. And just because God designed us to have a relationship with Him as his children does not make it easy for people to believe they can enter this spiritual kingdom.

Much like the tadpole that only begins to understand its future life when it first crawls out of the pond onto the shore, so we can only understand God's kingdom by stepping into it as a spiritual person.

Paul describes this difficulty when he says,

> *"No one knows the thoughts of a man except the man's spirit within him. In the same way, no one knows the thoughts of God except the Spirit of God. The man without the Spirit does not accept the things that come from the Spirit of God, for they are foolishness to him, and he cannot understand them, because they are spiritually discerned."*
>
> I Corinthians 2:11, 14

David could no more comprehend what Lemuel was saying about the secret kingdom than a tadpole could understand what the frog meant when he spoke of catching flies and breathing fresh air.

Like Lemuel, other people can explain the existence of the secret kingdom and share stories of what they have experienced there. But you cannot know it until you go there and experience it yourself.

If the tadpole never leaves the water, it will never know the life of a frog on dry ground. How do we know that we have left the world of the pond and entered the kingdom of the Spirit?

In exactly the same way a frog knows it is no longer a water dwelling tadpole. Everything changes—and the change is real.

The frog breaths differently than the tadpole; the frog eats differently than the tadpole; and the frog moves differently than the tadpole. The old life is gone and everything is new when the frog emerges from the water to live in its new kingdom on dry land.

It is the same when a person enters God's kingdom. Everything changes. It's like everything is experienced in a new way. A new life begins that is different from the life they lived before.

Like a frog learning to absorb oxygen through its lungs instead of its gills, a person learns to find truth through the Spirit of God speaking to them through the Bible and prayer. As the frog learns to eat bugs and insects on land, the new member of God's kingdom learns to nurture their spiritual life by what God teaches in the Bible, what they learn in church and what they learn by listing to God when they pray.

My friend Beth came to talk one day and asked how she could know if she was a Christian or not. I asked her the frog question.

"How is your life different now from the way it was before you decided to be part of God's kingdom?"

"Well, I go to church now," Beth replied, "and I am involved with the things we do in the singles ministry there."

"What has God been saying to you in your personal Bible study and prayer times?" I asked.

"I've been too busy for that," she said. "I'm overloaded at work and with all of the activities at church, I just don't have time. I'm exhausted when I get home each day."

"Are there things in your life that God has shown you should change but you have refused to change yet?" I asked.

Beth got quiet. "I guess I really haven't been living much of a spiritual life other than going to church."

Beth and I talked about David and the tadpoles; how David decided he did not want to be stuck in the human tadpole pond anymore. He wanted to step into God's spiritual kingdom and learn to live as on of God's children.

"That's what I want too," Beth admitted. "But I just don't know how to get there from here."

"Just do what David did," I said. "Tell God exactly how you feel and what you want. Admit to Him that you have done things wrong and ask Him to forgive you—He already wants to. Tell Him you want to really become one of His children and ask Him to show you what to do."

When a tadpole becomes a frog, the changes in its life are real. Once he becomes a frog, he never goes back to being a tadpole again. He must learn to live a new life. The old life is gone.

In the same way, the changes in our lives that happen when we enter God's spiritual kingdom are real, substantial and permanent. We must actually learn to hear and obey what God says to us. We must learn to live a new, spiritual life.

It takes a while for the tadpole to become a frog—it's a process. It gradually grows legs, becomes a polliwog and eventually loses all of the old water- dwelling characteristics. When we enter God's kingdom, we don't become totally spiritual over night. We go through process of change like the tadpole becoming a frog.

But never forget that the change is real.

> *"So from now on we regard no one from a worldly point of view . . .If anyone is in Christ, he is a new creation; the old has gone, the new has come."*
>
> II Corinthians 5:16, 17

SPIRITUAL EXERCISE

At the beginning of any trip, it is necessary to take out the map and mark the route you intend to follow. The first step is to find on the map exactly where you are now. In order to make the trip from the kingdom of this world into the kingdom of God, you must determine your starting point.

This exercise only works if you are honest with yourself. We will determine where you are today compared to where you want to be.

Spiritual Exercise, Part I: First, evaluate how you measure up to some of the qualities that God tells us define a spiritual versus an unspiritual life. On the left will be a lifestyle factor that God indicates does not fit within the plan of His kingdom. On the right will be a comparable character quality or behavior that He indicates you should find when living in the spiritual kingdom.

Put a circle around where you are today on the continuum between the two listed behaviors.

Sexual immorality; Sensuality, Lust	1-2-3-4-5-6-7-8-9-10	Sexual purity; Clean thoughts
Jealousy; Hatred; Anger	1-2-3-4-5-6-7-8-9-10	Forgiveness; Mercy; Peace
Drunkenness; Drugs; Addiction	1-2-3-4-5-6-7-8-9-10	Self-control; Healthy Habits; Self-control
Narcissism; Humanism; Selfishness	1-2-3-4-5-6-7-8-9-10	Focus on others; Compassion
Criticism; Gossip; Negative conversation	1-2-3-4-5-6-7-8-9-10	Affirmation; Encouragement; Supportiveness

Desire for sin;	1-2-3-4-5-6-7-8-9-10	Total love of
Pornography;		God; and Love
Love of things		for other people

When you measure your own heart by these Biblical guidelines, remember Paul's instruction: "Do not think more highly than you ought, but rather think of yourself with sober judgment, in accordance with the measure of faith God has given you." Romans 12:3.

Does your score on the self-test above tell you that you are living in God's spiritual kingdom or that you are still living in the kingdom of the world?

It may be time to get out of the water of this world and leave the life of the tadpole behind. It may be time to go deeper into God's spiritual kingdom where life is transformed by living close to Him.

If you find yourself drifting along the left side of this scale, go back and renew your commitment to live in God's kingdom. Talk to Him honestly, just like David did as he prayed by the pond with Lemuel.

Jesus clearly stated that it is God's will for you to be a part of His kingdom. He's waiting for you to come in right now. The door is open.

Knowing God is like knowing anyone else—it's a relationship. Relationships grow and change as two people get to know each other—like the tadpole becoming a frog. The change is real, but life in the sun beats being stuck in the water as a tadpole for the rest of your life.

CHAPTER FIVE

EXPECT IT TO RAIN

---

*"No discipline seems pleasant at the time,
but painful. Later on, however,
it produces a harvest of righteousness and
peace for those who have been trained by it."*
Hebrews 12:11

David's birthday was just a few weeks away and he was excited about planning his party. Lemuel said he could invite his friends from the city to come visit him on the farm for the weekend.

"You can be in charge of planning for the party," Lemuel said. "Make a list of all the things you think your friends will enjoy doing on the farm."

David spent all afternoon working on his list:

- Ride horses out to the pasture in the morning and have a picnic lunch;

- Swim in the fishing pond in the afternoon and sail the home-made boats on the pond;
- Build a bonfire behind the house on Saturday night so he could show his friends what he had learned about building fires;
- Cook hotdogs and s'mores on the fire.

"This is going to be the best birthday party ever!" David declared as he showed the list to Lemuel.

It was a Friday night when David's friends began to arrive. He told them stories all evening about his adventures on the farm and all the new things he had learned.

"You guys are going to have so much fun tomorrow!" he told them. "I've got the best day ever planned for us."

The boys were so excited they couldn't go to sleep. They played and talked until after midnight.

It was 8:00 o'clock when David woke up but it seemed too dark outside. His heart sank when he went to the window and looked outside. Dark clouds covered the farm like a wool blanket and it was starting to rain.

"All my plans are ruined," he said. "This is the worst birthday ever!"

"What are we going to do, Grandma?" David asked. "It's raining and we can't do anything."

"Let's start with a big farm breakfast and then figure out what to do after that," Lemuel answered calmly.

David didn't think she was taking this problem seriously enough, but those breakfasts were hard to beat. Just as they finished up a feast of ham, sausage, bacon, eggs and grits, Esron came in from the barn.

"Alright boys, get your rain coats on, we're going to the barn," he declared.

Esron showed the boys how to curry the horses and handle the tack. After they had each had a turn combing the horses, they all climbed the ladder into the haymow.

Esron had pile the hay up against the back wall like a mountain and brought them three big pieces of cardboard to use as sleds on their new indoor hill.

The morning flew by as they laughed and rolled down the mountain of hay over and over again.

"Hey boys," Lemuel said as he appeared at the top of the ladder. I've brought you a special haymow picnic!" she said.

Before he knew it, the day was over and it was time to go clean up for dinner. Before dinner, Lemuel had the boys come to the kitchen to help make cookies and to decorate David's cake. David watched his friends laughing as they cut different shapes into the cookie dough for the party.

He suddenly realized that Lemuel and Esron had planned things to do in case it was a rainy day.

"How did you know it was going to rain today?" David asked.

"Well, David," Lemuel replied, "I didn't know it was going to rain today, but the weatherman said it might. So Esron and I were ready just in case."

"Thanks Grandma, I'm glad you thought of that," David said as he gave her a hug. "It's the best birthday I've ever had."

After playing all day, the boys were tired after dinner and Lemuel sat them down and told them a story of two boys from the Bible—Daniel and Joseph.

"When Daniel was only twelve years old, just one year older than some of you, soldiers from another country came and took him from his family to be a slave in Babylon."

"He was far away from home in a place where everyone talked a different language, dressed in strange clothes and ate different food than he was used to.

"Daniel's mother had taught him to eat natural, healthy foods and to avoid things that would harm his body. In Babylon, his owners wanted him to eat rich, unhealthy food and drink wine with his meals."

"Was Daniel scared?" one of the boys asked.

"I'm sure he was," Lemuel answered.

"But even though he was scared and in a place he did not know, Daniel decided to stick up for what he had been taught at home before he was taken away to be a slave. He went to his boss and said he only wanted to eat simple natural food and drink no wine, just water. He asked to be given just as much work as any of the other slave boys."

"Watch me and see if I become weaker or stronger than the other boys" he said. "Then you will see if my diet is okay"

"His boss was nervous," Lemuel explained, "But he gave Daniel a chance to try his simple diet. He was surprised a few weeks later to see that Daniel was stronger and had more energy than the other boys."

"Was it hard being a slave?" David asked.

"Yes, it was," Lemuel said. "I think Daniel missed his family a lot."

"He had learned as a young boy to expect problems in life. His mother taught him that there would be rainy days when things didn't go as planned. But his mother taught him that the rain is just as important as the sunshine. God gives both of them to us so that things can grow."

"Why would God want to give us problems?" one of the boys asked.

"Why did God let it rain today?" Lemuel asked in response.

"Well, we need rain for things to grow," one boy volunteered. Another added, "Without the rain, everything would die."

"Life is kind of like that too," Lemuel explained, "Without problems, struggles and challenges we would never grow strong and learn to do what is right. The problems made Daniel stronger because he had to overcome them."

"Remember what happened to our other boy, Joseph, when he was a boy?" she asked.

"He had a fancy coat," one boy said.

"That's right. And his brothers were jealous of him because he was a favorite of his father."

"One day his brothers caught him out in the field, and kidnapped him and sold him to some people going to Egypt—like a slave," she explained.

"I'll bet he was really mad at them!" David said.

"Not as much as you'd expect," Lemuel said. "We read in the Bible how Joseph understood that just because something bad happened to him, it didn't mean God didn't still have a good plan for him."

"When they got to Egypt, he was sold as a slave to a rich family. He worked hard and did everything that he was told to do just as if it had been his father asking him to do something."

"He decided not to be angry or bitter toward his brothers because he knew there must be some reason God had let him be taken to Egypt. Just like the rain storm can help the crops grow, sometimes bad things can make good things happen later in our lives."

"Joseph worked really hard and kept getting promoted until he became the right-hand man to the king of Egypt. He was in charge of managing the king's money and possessions. Things got really bad back at home where his brothers lived because there was no rain. It was Joseph who was able to save them because he had become a ruler in Egypt. He sold them food to take back to their family in Israel."

"Oh, so it's kind of like getting prepared ahead of time in case it's a rainy day," David said with a smile. By now, he knew that Lemuel's stories always had a lesson in them.

"Exactly, David," Lemuel said. "Every person has problems to solve; disappointments to experience; and discipline to be learned. Stormy days never seem pleasant at the time, but God uses those things to teach us how to depend on Him, how to pray and how to work through problems with his help."

"You should expect rainy days, hard times and trouble in life. When bad things do happen, remember Daniel and Joseph—how God used the bad things to put each of them right where He needed them later so they could do important things for Him. They both realized that God was still there, even when they were in the middle of the storm. They kept on walking close to God until the storm was over and they ended up right where they were supposed to be."

APPLYING THE LESSON

Because Lemuel knew the value of expecting rainy days, she was able to plan rainy day activities for David and his friends. When storms come, they disrupt the lives of those who are unprepared.

Sometimes, as with Daniel, the test may be to indulge in pleasures that are not good for the body, mind or soul and which conflict with your inner moral integrity. What Daniel faced may not seem so serious at first but it can have major long-term consequences. Daniel understood that indulgence was disobedience and harmful to himself. He resisted the pressure of society to become a Babylonian couch potato.

The life Daniel chose was more difficult and disciplined than what everyone else around him was doing—but it worked. Because he chose what was best for himself in the long term, he ended up ahead of his competitors. He walked through the storm of criticism to the path of success.

It was a similar choice for Joseph. He had every right to be angry and bitter toward his brothers. What they did was wrong, painful and unfair. But instead, he chose to stand firm in his beliefs and build the new life that God had planned for him in Egypt.

Just like Joseph, a lot of people today are hurt, rejected and abused by people whom they trusted—sometimes members of their own family just like Joseph. Joseph shows us not only how to survive when these bad things happens, he shows us how succeed. The choices he made in his life show us how to survive painful, rainy days and come out on top when the sun shines again.

When feelings of pain and betrayal flood the soul, we face the same choices that Daniel and Joseph had to make. Will we spend our energy blaming the ones who hurt us or turn to the future and build a new life? Will we try to get revenge and hurt the ones who hurt us? Joseph said no to that option and as a result was able to save his whole family years later.

Thomas á Kempis writes:

> *"It is good for a man to suffer the adversity of this earthly life; for it brings him back to the sacred rest of the heart, where he finds his is an exile from his native home, and cannot place his trust in any worldly enjoyment. It is good for him also to meet with contradiction and reproach; and to be evil thought of, and evil spoken of, even when his intentions are right, and his actions blameless; for this keeps him humble, and is a powerful antidote to the poison of vanity."*

Modern society bombards us with messages that tell us that if we buy the right product, eat the right food, attend the right school, dress the right way and do the right exercises, life will be smooth and easy. Even churches often imply that if we just believe the right doctrine, follow the right teaching, and avoid a list of 'bad' things, life will be pleasant and the road ahead smooth.

Modern philosophy has idealized man's desire for hedonistic fulfillment to be an attainable result of right thinking and 'correct' behavior.

Daniel and Joseph teach us a different lesson. These two boys did everything right but bad things still happened to them.

Jesus did not teach a message of escape from the painful realities of life, but an invitation to let Him walk with you through those storms. You don't have to endure the stormy days by yourself. When the storm is over, you will still find God's plan is waiting for you just like Daniel and Joseph.

> *"I have told you these things, so that in me you may have peace. In this world you will have trouble."*
>
> John 16:33

You will face rainy, stormy days in your life. It is much better to be prepared for them ahead of time instead of waiting until after the rain starts. Get your spiritual umbrella ready now.

As James explained:

> *"Consider it pure joy, my brothers, whenever you face trials of many kinds, because you know that the testing of your faith develops perseverance. Perseverance must finish its work so that you may be mature and complete, not lacking anything."*
>
> James 1:2

Those who prepare before the storm begins emerge stronger after it has passed.

SPIRITUAL EXERCISE

Most of us avoid looking back on painful experiences from our past because it is difficult and uncomfortable. It's easier to just avoid it.

But the prophet tell us to, "break up your unplowed ground . . ." Jeremiah 4:9.

We can become hard and unproductive on the inside if we grow hard in the places where we have been hurt and disappointed in the past. Just like the ground needs to be plowed in the spring after the harsh winter has passed, we must break up the hard spots in our souls to allow for new growth.

The prophet Hosea tells us the same thing:

> *"Sow for yourselves righteousness, reap the fruit of unfailing love, and break up your unplowed ground; for it is time to seek the Lord, until he comes and showers righteousness on you."*
>
> Hosea 10:12

In this spiritual exercise, we will be looking back at painful events that may have created hard places in the soil of our hearts. The purpose of "breaking up the unplowed ground" is to prepare it for God to plant the seeds of your future there.

When I would go out to the garden in the spring after the frost came out of the ground, I'd find rocks, weeds and hard packed ground that needed to be broken up and prepared for planting. Nothing would grow until the garden was prepared.

Spiritual Exercise, Part I: In the space provided below or on a separate piece of paper, write out the three events or experiences from your past that caused you the most pain, trouble or anger. Be specific about what happened—who did it, what happened, and why did it happen.

1. _____

2. _____

3. _____

Now review how you felt and responded to each of these three events when they happened to you.

Pray this simple prayer as you look back at your behavior: *"Father, open my spiritual eyes to see how my response to this event reflected or failed to reflect Your spiritual character in me."*

1. _____

2. _____

3. _____

You may find within the soil of your soul stones of anger and roots of bitterness over past offenses; we will discuss them in chapter that follow.

Finally, look back at these three painful experiences. Write down how these negative events have made you stronger, wiser or more capable of dealing with problems you encounter in your life.

1. _____

2. _____

3. _____

Spiritual Exercise, Part II: Lemuel taught David the importance of expecting the stormy days and preparing before they arrive. Peter gives us a similar instruction:

> *"Therefore, prepare your minds for action . . .*
> *"Be self-controlled and alert. Your enemy the*
> *devil prowls around like a roaring lion looking*
> *for someone to devour. Resist him."*
> I Peter 1:13; 5:8

We have looked back at three storms from your past. Now it is time to your future. It's time to be prepared for the next storm that comes.

Look briefly at each major area of your life—your walk with God, your marriage and family, your job, and your life goals. What possible storms might you encounter on the road ahead?

At work, for example, you might get a boss or supervisor who is angry or hard to work for or who makes demands you can't accept, like what happened to Daniel. At home, conflict might develop between you and your spouse or one of your children. In your walk with God, you may face temptation to do things that will harm you in the long term. These are all storms you might have to walk through in the future.

Spiritual Exercise, Part III: First, select three important areas of your life. In Part A, write down a storm you might encounter in that part of your life. Then, in Part B, consider what an effective, Godly response would be to that negative event.

What could you do to remain close to God if that storm arrived? Mentally prepare solutions to potential problems before they happen. We all hope they never do. But we all encounter some storms along the way. The more you have developed the skill of getting through them strong in your walk with God, the better prepared you will be when they arrive.

Life Area 1:

A. Possible painful or negative event:

_____

B. Godly response/solution:

_____

Life Area 2:

A. Possible painful or negative event:

_____

B. Godly response/solution:

_____

Life Area 3:

A. Possible painful or negative event:

_____

B. Godly response/solution:

_____

As you consider the storms from the past, work to clear the ground of debris left behind. Break up the hard spots and open up the soil of your heart to the new things God has to plant there. You may need to forgive someone; start a new habit; end an old habit; change some relationships and refocus some areas of your life.

That's what springtime is all about—renewing the soil so something new can grow.

Be prepared for the next storm that comes. And it _will_ come. Know where to find shelter close to God in the middle of the rain. Be prepared to respond to struggle the way Daniel and Joseph did.

Enjoy the sunshine God gives you but be ready in case it rains tomorrow.

CHAPTER SIX

LOST IN THE WOODS

"Happiness is a direction,
not a place."
Sydney J. Harris

D avid's favorite birthday gift was a new Remington .22 caliber rifle.

After dinner, before the sun went down, Esron would take David out to the sand pit to practice and learn how to use his gun safely.

Esron put up six old tin cans on a board and let David shoot until he'd hit them all. By the end of the week, David was getting bored with shooting cans.

"I know how to shoot now," David said. "Let's go hunting!"

Esron made him practice for one more week and then agreed to take him squirrel hunting in the north forest. That night David could barely sleep.

As they finished up breakfast and packed a sandwich for lunch, David said, "Don't cook until I get home, Grandma. I'm going hunting for our supper."

The north forest was full of grey squirrels that loved to feast on the acorns from the big oak trees. After reviewing the safety rules, Esron loaded the gun and David took aim at his first target.

Pow! The gun went off, but the squirrel just ran off to another tree.

"What happened, Grandpa?" David asked. "I missed the squirrel."

"Sometimes real life is harder than practice," Esron noted. "The squirrels aren't going to sit still like your tin cans did."

David shot his way though a whole box of shells and didn't hit a squirrel. He stopped for lunch, a little disappointed in his marksmanship.

After lunch, Esron took a turn and quickly dropped a couple of squirrels, cleaned them and wrapped them in the plastic bags they had brought to keep them clean.

Esron was getting a little tired, so he sat down by a big log to rest awhile and David wandered off into the woods nearby to explore—he wasn't going to spend his afternoon sitting around!

"You can go explore," Esron said, "but you must stay close enough to always see that big pine tree at the edge of the clearing."

"Okay," David said, as he bounded into the woods.

Esron soon dozed off in the warm afternoon sun and you can guess what happened next.

That's right: David got lost.

He spotted a big, snowshoe rabbit and stalked it deeper and deeper into the woods. A few minutes later, he realized he had no idea where he was or how to get back to the clearing where Esron was sleeping. He couldn't see the big pine tree any more.

He climbed a tree to see if that helped, but still no big pine tree in sight. Now he was scared—he was lost and he didn't know how to find his way back.

"Esron! Where are you?" David yelled as loud as he could.

Esron woke up and could just barely hear David's voice off in the distance. He smiled just a little as he remembered some his own adventures in the forest as a boy. He knew how David felt.

Then Esron did something unusual; he stared to sing. In a rich baritone voice, he started to sing one of his favorite songs about sometimes feeling lost in the world: *"I'm just a poor wayfaring stranger. A passin' through this land of woe . . ."*

David heard Grandpa start to sing and suddenly felt safe again. He could tell exactly what direction to go to get back to Grandpa. He really wasn't as lost as he thought he was. It was easy to follow Esron's voice back to the clearing, where he got a big hug.

"It's pretty scary getting lost, isn't it?" Esron said.

"It sure is!" David said. "I didn't know where I was until I heard you sing."

David and Esron decided to hunt just a little longer before going home. With a little help from Esron, David finally got his first squirrel. David would remember his first hunting trip for a long time.

As they walked out of the woods, Esron showed David how to pick out a tree in the distance as a landmark and how to maintain a straight line in the woods by lining up two trees in the direction he was heading.

"It's important to always keep your eyes on where you are going," Esron explained. "If you don't watch where you are going, you will never get there.

"When you get older your life will be full of work, family and responsibility. There will be days when there is so much going on that it will be easy to get lost and forget the direction of your life.

"Those are the days when you must remember to keep your eyes on the landmarks you have chosen to keep your life going in the right direction. It's easy to wander off the path like you did today and get lost in life."

"I know what the most important thing is to aim at," David said proudly.

"What's that?" Esron asked.

"It's to be a friend of God's—like Grandma always says."

"Good answer," Esron said. "And if you keep your eyes on Jesus, it will be easy to find God's plan for your life."

"Can I hear Him sing if I get lost?" David asked with a laugh.

"Well, He might not sing for you," Esron replied, "but if you stop where you are and say, 'Jesus, I'm lost. I can't find my way back to the path.' You will hear His voice just like you heard mine in the woods. If you follow the sound of that voice like you did when you heard me singing, it will always lead you back to the path of life you were on."

"You're almost as smart as Grandma," David laughed as he gave Esron a little hug.

Esron smiled. The two men had formed a special bond on their hunting trip that day. "Sometimes being a little lost helps us appreciate how nice it is to be found," Esron thought.

"You know David," Esron observed, "perhaps the best thing about getting lost in the woods is that you have learned how important it is in your life to keep moving in the same direction every day—always keeping your eyes on God."

APPLYING THE LESSON

A team of climbers recently celebrated as they reached the top of Mt. Everest. They all called home on their satellite cell phones to share the good news. The local papers carried glowing reports of their success. But good news suddenly turned to tragedy as they were caught in a sudden blizzard on the way down the mountain and lost the path. Nine climbers died on the mountain that day in the shadow of yesterday's success.

It does no good to attain success if you cannot find the pathway back home at the end of the day.

David did not realize how easy it was to get lost when he wandered away from the clearing in the woods. In just a few minutes, he could no longer see the clearing and he began to walk in circles in the woods.

Fortunately, David realized he was lost before he had wandered too far away from the clearing to hear Esron's voice. It is easy for urgent tasks, busyness, fun, fear or wrong relationships to lead us away from the path we have set for ourselves in life. Soon we find ourselves surrounded by a forest of problems, concerns, and failures that obscure the path of our life's purpose.

In the Bible we see this happening to one of Paul's student's, Demus. Paul writes: *"Demus has forsaken me, having loved this present world."* Demus took his eyes of his path to God and ended up getting lost in the forest of earthly desire—a sad but frequently repeated problem today as well.

Jesus used the picture of a farm field where the crop had been infected with weeds and thorny vines. He tells how the "cares of this world" had choked the life out of the crop until the field became useless.

David heard Esron's voice carry through the woods as he sang. Even though he was lost, he responded to that voice and followed it back to safety. Just like David, we need to stop and listen for the voice that will lead us back to safety when we have wandered from the path of God's plan for our lives.

When he was lost, David had to walk the full distance back to the clearing where he would be safe. When you hear the voice, follow it until you get all the way back home.

SPIRITUAL EXERCISE

Jesus said that the pathway to God is narrow and hard to find—"Only a few find it." It's easy to get lost in the spiritual woods and wander so far away we can't hear God's voice calling us back.

In earlier lessons, we began to work on developing our ability to hear and listen to God's voice. In this lesson, we will start to define and identify the narrow path that leads to God and how to find landmarks along the trail.

The key landmarks that mark the pathway to God are righteousness, faithfulness and truth. In a world of relativism, self-interest and the pursuit of pleasure, God's landmarks stand out in contrast to the direction most of the world is traveling.

Because God's kingdom is spiritual, it can only be seen with the eyes of your spirit. Jesus once said, "I tell you the truth, unless a man is born of the Spirit he cannot see the kingdom of God."

Spiritual Exercise, Part I: Finding God's Landmarks.

In the space below, list six landmarks that distinguish the way of God from the way of the world. For example, the world says, "Practice safe sex," but God says, "Practice sexual purity." When I am deep in the forest and stumble onto a path of sexual opportunity, I can look at God's landmark of righteousness—sexual purity—and follow it back to where God wants me to be. Other landmarks of righteousness might be honesty, integrity, trust in God, forgiveness, generosity and compassion.

Spend a few minutes in prayer before you begin and ask God to show you the landmarks of His righteousness that are relevant and important to your path. List those six landmarks below.

Landmarks of Righteousness

    1. _____

    2. _____

3. _____

4. _____

5. _____

6. _____

Spiritual Exercise, Part II: Landmarks of Faithfulness.

Landmarks of righteousness are objective, external landmarks that tell us if we are on God's path or not. Landmarks of faithfulness relate to whether our relationships with other people are right or not.

In each of the three examples below, describe the choice, which represents faithfulness in relationships consistent with God's landmarks.

Example 1: Lynn has been married for six years and has three children at home. The last couple of years have been hard because her husband has had to work late several nights each week and likes to play golf or go fishing on the weekend. She feels alone as she rushes home every night to make dinner, care for the house and take care of chores.

Now one of the salesmen at the office has been taking her out to lunch and she enjoys the attention. She is sure he wants more.

She is committed to her family but she feels lonely and hungry inside, and likes the attention. Lynn is getting lost in the forest of loneliness and desire. What landmarks of God can she look to that will help her keep her life on track?

_____

_____

_____

Example 2: Chet was in trouble at work. He has been overwhelmed with projects for the last several months and has made a couple of big mistakes. Today, he found a project with an important deadline buried on his desk that he had forgotten.

Now, it's caught up with him and he's in trouble.

Chet is afraid because he knows his boss is going to be angry. This could cost him his job. He has two choices: he could blame the oversight on his assistant, or he could take the heat himself.

He has seen other managers blame mistakes on their staff and get through problems like this without getting fired. Of course, he knew it wasn't really his assistant's fault—he had forgotten it himself.

What landmarks of faithfulness can Chet look to in order to keep him on God's path instead of getting lost in the forest of deceit?

_____

_____

_____

Example 3: As a married couple, Megan and Harold had become best friends with Trey and Beth. Every week they would do something together—cook dinner, go camping, or watch the big game. Then Megan and Harold got divorced and that created a problem— Megan didn't seem to fit into Beth's plans anymore. She was upset and bitter about the divorce. She spent all of her time complaining when they talked.

Beth began to wonder if she should just let Megan go as a friend and not include her in activities anymore. What landmarks of faithfulness can Beth use to navigate her way to a Godly answer to this problem?

_____

_____

_____

Spiritual Exercise, Part III: Landmarks of Truth.

In addition to right conduct, called" righteousness," and right relationships, called "faithfulness," God gives us landmarks of truth. For example, if I am lost in the woods early in the morning, I know the sun will be low in the sky to the east. It is a landmark I can use to find direction. In the same way, God has given us certain 'guiding principles' to give us direction as we plot our course through life.

Here are four of these landmarks. Write them each on a card you can carry with you and review them until you have memorized each principle.

Then ask God to show you how to use them when you need them.

Landmark of Truth, No. 1: "The soul that sinneth, it shall die." Ezekiel 18:20 (also see, I John 3:4-10).

Sin is like a poisonous drug. When we take it, it begins to kill our inner spirit and blind us to God's path. When we sin or feel the temptation to do what we know is wrong, we can look to this truth and understand that the consequences of sin are always bad for us.

Like a bad drug, it makes us feel good at first, but eventually we overdose and die spiritually.

Landmark of Truth, No. 2: You can never get lost so deep in the woods that God can't lead you back to Himself. "And be sure of this—that I am with you always even to the end of the world." Matthew 28:20.

You can never wander so far from God that He can't bring you back. There is always an open door at His house. Satan will tell you you're too much of a failure to ever go back home—God disagrees.

Landmark of Truth, No. 3: God is willing to forgive any sin for which you are willing to take responsibility and which you are willing to stop. "If we confess our sins, He is faithful and just to forgive us our sins and to purify us from all unrighteousness." I John 1:9.

Regardless of how deep you wander into the darkness of the woods, remember this landmark: God wants to forgive you and bring you back to His place. He misses your friendship.

Landmark of Truth, No. 4: If I blame others and refuse to forgive them, it prevents God from forgiving me. "For if you forgive men when they sin against you, your heavenly Father will also forgive you. But if you do not forgive men their sins, your Father will not forgive your sins." Matthew 6:14, 15.

Jesus explained this principle like this: "For in the same way you judge others, you will be judged, and with the measure you use, it will be measured to you." Matthew 7:1, 2.

That seems fair, doesn't it? When you feel a rising sense of anger, unforgiveness or bitterness, look to this landmark as a guide to show you how God wants you to respond.

David got lost in the woods because he lost sight of the landmark Esron had given him. He was smart enough to follow Esron's when he began to sing. When you find you have wandered from the path you were on, stop and listen for God's voice and follow it until you get back to where He is waiting for you.

CHAPTER SEVEN

THE DANGERS OF THE DARK

"Body and soul contain a thousand possibilities
out of which you can build many I's.
But in only one of them is there congruence
of the elector and the elected."
Dag Hammarskjold, *Markings*

On Monday afternoon, Lemuel asked David to help her bake a batch of chocolate-chip oatmeal cookies for the women's circle that meet on Tuesday mornings. They were David's favorite. Lemuel had gotten the recipe from her mother when she was a girl. She even won the blue ribbon at the county fair three times with her chewy temptations.

David mixed the brown sugar and molasses together with a little milk and melted butter. The mixture smelled rich and sweet. David's stomach began to growl.

"Let's hurry up and cook these," David said. I'm hungry!"

"We'll make a few extra so that you can have a couple," Lemuel responded. "But remember, these are not for you to eat. They are for the circle tomorrow."

"You'd better make a lot then," David replied. "I could eat them all myself."

They added several cups of oatmeal to the cookie dough and David mixed in the chocolate chips. He helped Lemuel spoon the dough out onto the cookie sheets; one dozen balls of temptation on each pan.

When the last of the cookies were scooped onto the cookie sheets, David volunteered to scrape out the bowl with a spatula and lick the spoon.

Lemuel put the first pan of cookies into the oven and began to clean up. David could smell the cookies as they baked. His mouth watered.

"Are they done yet?" he asked, opening the oven to take a peek.

"Keep the door closed or they won't cook right," Lemuel answered. "I'll set the timer for you. They still have ten minutes to go."

As soon as the timer went off, David opened the oven door and grabbed a cookie.

"Ouch!" He yelled as he jerked back his hand. "They're hot!"

Lemuel didn't even answer him. She just shook her head and picked up the hot-pad to take the pan out of the oven. One by one she placed the cookies on the cooling rack on the counter. David couldn't stand it. It seemed as if she took forever. He wanted a cookie now!

"Can I have one now?" he asked.

"Not yet," Lemuel responded. "Let them cool down first."

"I hate waiting," David said. "I'm hungry right now."

"Everything that is good comes only after you wait for it," Lemuel answered. "When Esron plants the seed in the springtime, he must wait all summer for a crop. When a mother becomes pregnant, she must wait nine months for the baby to be born. Someday, when you go to college, you will have to wait four years to get your degree. Everything good takes time to grow."

"Well, I still don't like waiting," David declared. "I don't want to wait for everything. It should be faster."

"Help me dry these dishes and put them away," Lemuel said. "You can test one of the cookies when you finish."

After they finished cleaning up, Lemuel carefully placed four of the warm cookies on a plate for David and said, "These are yours. The rest of the cookies we will save for the circle tomorrow. You can eat your cookies now or save them for later, but this is all you get."

By the time Lemuel had poured David a glass of milk, two of the cookies were already gone. The rest disappeared within minutes.

With his stomach now warm and happy, David went out to play with Luke and to help Esron with chores before supper.

After dinner, David asked, "Grandma, can I have a cookie for desert?"

"No," she answered. "We have to save the rest for tomorrow."

"But Grandma," David whined, "no one will ever notice if one more cookie is missing."

Lemuel ignored him and slowly got up to clear the table. David noticed that Lemuel seemed to be getting slower than she had been at the beginning of the summer. It sometimes made him feel sad inside, but he didn't know what to say about it.

After dinner, Esron got out his old guitar and sat in the living room singing old songs that David had never heard before. Some of the songs were fun, and David and Lemuel would sing along. Before bed, Lemuel always read David two or three stories from the Bible story book that she had used when her own three boys were young. She liked the memories tucked between the pages of the old book that she had used so long ago.

After he got his pajamas on, David asked, "Grandma, can I have just one cookie before I go to bed? Please!"

"I'm sorry," Lemuel answered. "We can make more another time, but we need to save these for tomorrow."

David didn't like that word, "no." His bottom lip stuck out, and he pouted his way upstairs to bed. As he lay there trying to go to sleep, he couldn't get the cookies out of his mind. It didn't seem fair that he couldn't have just one more cookie. After all, he had helped make them himself.

He heard Esron and Lemuel turn of the lights in the room next door and soon he heard Esron begin to snore. But David couldn't sleep. His mind was filled with pictures of warm, chocolate chip oatmeal cookies.

"I'll bet Grandma wouldn't notice if one cookie was missing," he said to himself.

He couldn't stand it any longer. He was just too hungry to go to sleep, and it wasn't fair for the ladies at church to get all the cookies he had made. Quietly, he slipped out from under the covers and tiptoed to the door. He could still hear Esron snoring, so he knew that Esron and Lemuel were asleep.

He was afraid she would catch him, but he slowly crept down the stairs. His heart was beating so hard in his chest that he was afraid it would wake up Lemuel. He flinched each time one of the old steps let out a little creak, like a burglar alarm warning of the prowling cookie thief.

When he finally got downstairs, he quietly slipped into the kitchen. It was dark and he couldn't see. But he knew his way around, so he felt his way over to the far wall where Lemuel kept the cookie jar. As he lifted off the lid, it gave a sharp "clink" that made David freeze and hold his breath. He listened to be sure that Esron and Lemuel were still asleep.

The house was so quiet that the only sound David could hear was the pounding of his heart. He reached in and retrieved his sweet reward. He stood there silently eating the fruit of his temptation. It tasted good. He quietly opened the refrigerator and took a drink of milk from the bottle—something Lemuel would never let him do when she was around. He smiled at the success of his mission.

"That was so good," he thought. *"Maybe I'll have just one more before Grandma takes them all to church."* He felt his way back to the cookie jar and reached in for one final stolen delight. It tasted just as good as the first one. He was getting sleepy now, and he knew that his snack would help him sleep.

One last drink of milk and he'd be on his way back to bed. As he put the lid back on the cookie jar, he decided to take one more cookie to eat on his way upstairs. He felt like a secret agent sneaking behind enemy lines on a spy mission. It was exciting.

David silently replaced the cover, picked up his last cookie and turned to sneak back upstairs. Two steps across the kitchen floor his foot suddenly hit a giant mound of sleeping fur. Luke was sleeping on the kitchen floor and David had not seen him in the dark.

David fell forward hitting his head on the edge of a kitchen chair. "Ouch!" he cried involuntarily. Startled, Luke let out a yelp and ran across the kitchen knocking over another chair with a bang.

David felt something on his forehead. It was wet.

He had cut himself on the chair when he fell. There he lay, with blood on his forehead and a smashed cookie in his hand. Esron came running through the door and turned on the light to see what had happened.

David was busted!

Lemuel came in right behind him.

"David, what happened?" she asked.

"The stupid dog was sleeping in the middle of the floor, and I tripped," David replied.

"It looks as if we have caught ourselves a clumsy thief," Esron said with a smile, as Lemuel wiped the blood from the cut on David's forehead.

"I just wanted to have one more cookie," David cried. "They were so good, and I helped make them myself. I'm sorry I didn't listen to what you said."

"It's dangerous to go walking around in the dark, isn't it?" Lemuel asked. "Why didn't you turn on the light?"

"I was afraid I would wake up you and Grandpa," David answered. You told me not to take any more cookies, and I didn't want you to find out."

"You felt safer in the dark because you knew what you were doing was wrong, didn't you?" Lemuel asked. "Did it seem okay to you if no one knew what you were doing?"

"I just didn't want to get caught," David said. "I knew I wasn't supposed to be down there."

"One day, when Jesus was explaining the spiritual kingdom to a leader of the Jews, He said the people don't want to come into the light when they feel that what they are doing is wrong," Lemuel explained. "And the people who are doing what is right are comfortable in the light because they know that they are doing what God wants them to do."

"I remember that," David said. "That was the Nicodemus guy that you told me about last week."

"That's right," Lemuel replied. "But what I want you to hear me say is that whenever you feel safer in the dark than with the lights on, you should check what is happening in your heart. You may be trying to hide from the light because you know that what you are doing is wrong."

"Yeah, I didn't want you to find out that I was taking more of your cookies," David answered. "I feel dumb now."

"It was wrong for you to take the cookies after you had been told no. But there will be a lot of other times in your life when you will want to do things that you know are wrong. The Bible calls those times temptation."

"I want you to think tonight and remember what happens when you want to do things you know you shouldn't do."

"I end up feeling pretty stupid, for one thing," David said.

"And you end up hurting yourself as well," Lemuel added. "You may not always trip and cut your head, but when you choose to walk in the darkness and do what God says is wrong, it always ends up hurting and embarrassing you sooner or later. The reason God said those things are wrong is because they end up hurting you."

"But I really wanted a cookie," David said. "I just couldn't' get it out of my head."

"How do you feel about it now?" Lemuel asked.

"I feel bad that I disappointed you and Grandpa and woke everybody up," David answered. "And, my head hurts."

"That's what I mean," Lemuel answered. "When you disobey, you will always end up hurt and disappointed. Remember the picture that Jesus gave you about walking in the light. When you want something, but you know it is wrong, close your eyes and ask God to turn on the light in your heart so that you don't stumble into the darkness and get hurt."

APPLYING THE LESSON

David faced a choice between right and wrong. He asked if he could have another cookie and was told no. He didn't like that answer, because he wanted to feel the taste of that chocolate and oatmeal melting in his mouth.

The more he thought about it, the more he wanted it. Temptation always works that way. Then he made a choice. He decided to sneak downstairs in the dark to take what he wanted even though he knew it was wrong—wanting it made it seem alright to him at the time.

When his friend Lazarus was sick, Jesus told His disciples that it was time to go to Bethany where Lazarus lived. They did not want to go because the Jews there had tried to stone Jesus the last time He was there.

Jesus' answer describes the other side of David's choice:

> *"There are twelve hours of daylight. A man who walks by day will not stumble, for he sees by the world's light. It is when he walks by night that he stumbles because he has no light."*
> John 11:9, 10.

The disciples wanted to play it safe and stay in Galilee where things were going well for them. But Jesus knew that He needed to go to Judea to see His friend, even if it wasn't the easy or safe thing to do. The decision about what is right or wrong to do is not based on the level of risk—it is based on the level of obedience.

It is only when we step outside of the spotlight of God's will that we need fear the darkness. The picture of light and darkness is a picture of walking with God or walking away from God; of choosing to do what

God says to do or choosing to do what we feel like doing—whatever we think will make us happiest.

Jesus said, "I am the light of the world. Whoever follows me will never walk in darkness, but will have the light of life." (John 8:1). Walking in the light means to stay close to Jesus and do what God has told us is right. Walking in the darkness means doing our own thing. It is acting outside of the boundaries of God's approval.

If we choose the path of darkness, we will always end up on the kitchen floor next to David with a bleeding head and the crumbs of sinful desire in our hands. Walking in the light works and walking in the dark doesn't.

When the desire of temptation seizes your heart, it will not feel as if this is true, but it is. David felt that the right thing to do was to slip down to the kitchen in the dark and sneak one extra cookie. David was wrong.

When we feel temptation rise to the surface of our hearts and start to pull us toward it, we need to retreat to the place in our soul close to God where we can walk in the light and say no to the darkness. Always walk with your back to the shadow.

> "From Me, the small and the great, the poor and the rich draw the water of life. But he who desires to glory in things outside of Me, or to take pleasure in some private good, shall not be grounded in true joy, or be enlarged in his heart, but shall in many ways be encumbered and restricted. For if in anything you seek yourself, immediately you faint and dry up in yourself."
> Thomas á Kempis, *The Imitation of Christ*

SPIRITUAL EXERCISE

*"When we have found God, there is nothing
more to look for in men. As God said to Abraham,
'Walk in My Presence, and you will be perfect.'"*
Francois Fenelon

The struggle to find God's will consumes far less of the Christian life than the struggle to do it. David saw in the bruises and embarrassment of the kitchen floor the truth that walking in the darkness eventually leads to pain and failure. In this exercise, we will seek to examine and define the line of separation between darkness and light and to examine what changes might be necessary to bring our behavior into the light of God's will.

When asked to describe the boundary between light and darkness, Jesus gave two answers. First, He said that the greatest act of obedience was to "Love the Lord your God with all your heart and with all your soul and with all your mind and with all your strength." (Mark 12: 30). On another occasion when the Jews asked Him, "what must we do to do what God requires?" Jesus answered, "The work of God is this: to believe in the one He has sent." (John 6:29).

The intersection of these two answers lies in the idea that to love God is to believe in the one He sent and that to believe in the one He sent is to love God. These two acts cannot be performed separately.

What follows from believing in Jesus and loving God is a life flooded with light from a God who is close by. As you do the following exercises, begin by speaking with the God who has chosen to make a dwelling place within you. Ask him to be the light close-by who directs your path away from darkness and even closer to the light—Himself.

Spiritual Exercise, Part I: Take paper or a notebook and find a place where you are free from interruption. Begin by making a complete list of those times when you have acted in ways that you knew were wrong. Even if you have already accepted God's forgiveness and worked through the consequences of those actions, list them here for purposes of review.

Write your list of experiences on the left-hand side of the page, leaving room on the right for the second part of this exercise. Examples of things that might appear on your list would be taking something that was not yours, saying something that was not true, entertaining angry or lustful thoughts in your mind, speaking to others in harmful ways, and/or acting selfishly when face with another person's needs. Make your list specific. Describe where and when each time you did something wrong.

After you have made a complete list of all the times when you chose to walk in darkness, take a few minutes to tell God that you regret your choices and that you don't want to repeat them in the future.

Ask Him to forgive you of all of these things and to clean your heart of the desire to ever do them again. Ask Him to clean up any mess that still remains in your heart as a result of these past sins.

> *"If we confess our sins, he is faithful and just and will forgive us our sins and purify us from all unrighteousness."*
>
> I John 1:9

Spiritual Exercise, Part II: After you have listed every act of darkness that you can remember and after you have talked to God about what you've done, ask God to help you see the consequences of your past actions.

David decided to steal a cookie and ended up with a cut forehead. What happened as a result of the things you have listed on the left hand side of your page? Did the sinful act that you chose to do lead to guilt, failure, damaged relationships, separation from God, emotional pain or some other dysfunctional outcome?

Look deeply enough to see the long-term consequences of each course of conduct you chose to walk. When I actually stop and see the consequences of wrong behavior, it helps motivate me to avoid it in the future. I want to stay away from the dark.

Spiritual Exercise, Part III: Finally, as the third part of this exercise, write down everything that God has ever asked you to do or change in your life which you have not yet acted upon. This may include things that you felt led to do while reading the Bible, listening to a sermon or praying. Include in this list those things which you have felt needed to be changed in your life when you prayed and looked into your own heart.

As you begin this exercise, wade into the pool of God's presence and ask Him to refresh your memory and bring to your mind the light that you have received but in which you have never walked.

Spend five minutes meditating on these acts of obedience that you still have to implement in your life. Ask God to help you imagine how it would change your life if you did each of these things that you have been asked to do.

Finally, ask God to give you the strength to take action. Pick one of the items on your list of unfinished acts of obedience and start it now. After it is finished, start on another one. Obedience will change your life.

"Immediately, when you obey, a flash of light comes. In spiritual relationship we do not grow step by step; we are either there or we are not. God does not cleanse us more and more from sin, but when we are in the light, walking in the light, we are cleansed from all sin. It is a question of obedience, and instantly the relationship is perfected. Turn away for one second out of obedience, and darkness and death are at work at once."

Oswald Chambers, *My Utmost For His Highest*

CHAPTER EIGHT

KEEP MOVING WEST

"They too stand in the sunlight,
but with their backs to the sun."
Kalil Gibran, *The Prophet*

Down the road three miles from Lemuel's farm lived a family with six children—three boys and three girls. Their son, Parez, was ten years old, just like David. Each week, Parez would come over and spend an afternoon playing with David.

David's birthday was last week and his favorite toy was a black, remote-controlled Dodge Ram pickup, which his parents had given him. He just about wore the tires off it in the first week! He'd race it up and down the driveway, practice turns, fishhooks and sudden stops. He was an expert driver by now.

So, when Parez came to visit, David proudly showed him his great new truck. They went outside so he could show Parez all of the tricks he had learned.

"You push the lever this way to make it go forward and then push it down to make it go backward," David explained. He explained all of the controls and drove the car up and down the driveway expertly avoiding every rock and pothole. He fish hooked at the end of the driveway and raced it back to the house.

"That looks fun!" Parez said. "Can I try it?"

David said, "Sure, you can try it, but it's hard to steer at first, be careful. Don't let it get away from you."

Parez practiced going forward slowly and then back. Soon he felt more confident and tried to race it down the driveway like David had done.

"Not so fast!" David yelled. "It will spin out!"

But David's warning came too late. The truck suddenly veered to the right, hit a rock and flew full speed into the big oak tree. It instantly shattered into pieces. The front axle went one way, the bumper another and the hood wouldn't stay closed any more.

David felt as if his heart had hit the tree. "That's my favorite truck," David said. He tried to act as if everything was okay, but a single tear rolled down his cheek, silently revealing his disappointment.

"I'm sorry," Parez said. "I didn't mean to break it."

David didn't say anything. He was angry that Parez had broken his favorite birthday present.

Later that night at dinner, David said, "I should never have let Parez play with my truck. I don't like him any more."

"I thought he was your friend," Lemuel said.

"Not any more!" David said firmly. "I liked that truck and he broke it."

"Well, if he was your friend this morning, where did that friendship go?" Lemuel asked.

"I don't want to talk about it. I'm mad." David snapped.

"Oh, I see," Lemuel said as she paused for a moment. "Does that help you feel better?"

"Better? I don't feel better. I'm mad! You just don't understand. It wasn't your truck." David said.

"You're right about that," Lemuel answered.

She sat quietly for a few minutes and then said, "When I was a little girl, my friend, Naomi, came to the ranch to stay for a week while her parents were out of town. Naomi and I each had one doll. As a little girl, my doll was my favorite possession.

"We played dolls together every day. One afternoon, my mom called me to come help her fix dinner. Naomi stayed outside and played with our dolls. When she came in for supper, she forgot my doll under the same oak tree that your truck hit. It rained during dinner that night and my only doll was ruined.

"At first I was angry, just like you are now. But my mother talked to me for a long time that night. She told me about a power that God gives us to erase things that hurt us so they don't keep on hurting us in the future. She said that forgiveness is love's secret weapon."

"Love?" said David. "I don't want to love Parez. I'm mad at him. He broke my truck."

"Yes, he did," Lemuel replied, "but does that have to change you?"

"It makes me mad. That's what it does," said David.

"What if, inside of your mind, you could go back and erase what happened today? Would you and Parez be friends then?"

"Well, I suppose we would be," David answered. "But my truck's still broken and I can't erase that."

"In the Bible, King David once wrote a song about forgiveness," Lemuel answered. "In his song he wrote that God removes the memory of the bad things we have done 'as far away as the east is from the west.'

If you went outside and walked west toward the barn, and then kept walking west, how far would you have to go before you came out on the east side of the farm?"

"I would never come out on the east side of the farm if I keep walking west," David answered.

"That's right," said Lemuel. "If we put the painful things that other people do to us to the east of us and then turn west and walk away, we leave the pain, anger and memory of what happened behind us. If we keep moving west, we keep walking farther and farther away from what hurt us. Because we keep walking forward, the hurt that we felt keeps getting farther and farther away from us until it's gone."

"But what Parez did was wrong," David protested.

"Yes, he was careless, and that is what broke your truck," Lemuel agreed. "The power of forgiveness lets us move past the pain of what happened. It's like a secret weapon. It lets you move forward when other people would get stuck and bogged down in the past."

"How would you feel if I reminded you every day of every bad thing you have ever done? If you could never get away from the bad things *you* did in the past?" Lemuel asked.

"I'd be in big trouble if that happened," David said. "I guess I would feel better if I wasn't mad at Parez."

"You're right about that," Lemuel said. "The Bible tells us that love does not keep a record of wrongs. It erases the hurt when it happens by putting it behind and walking over to the comforting arms of God."

"You're pretty smart, Grandma," David said with a smile. "I guess I will feel better if I let Parez be my friend again. In fact, I feel a little better already. Does that mean I've started to walk west?" He said with a smile.

David was still sad that his truck was broken. He missed playing with it. But now, each time he walked past the old oak tree or saw the broken truck in his room, he remembered what Lemuel had said about putting what happened behind him and moving forward in life.

"It feels good to walk west," he thought. He wasn't mad any more.

After a couple of weeks, David didn't think about the truck any more. He felt stronger because he had learned how to forgive.

"You were right, Grandma," he said. "The farther I walk away from what made me mad, the better I feel inside. It doesn't hurt inside any more like it did at first."

APPLYING THE LESSON

David felt pain, disappointment and loss when his truck hit the tree. Something he valued had been taken away from him. It was personal, like something inside of him was broken, not just the truck. There will be days when you feel like David—when hopes, dreams and plans for the future shatter against the unexpected reality of today's oak tree.

My first impulse when I feel disappointment caused by someone else's carelessness or cruelty is to blame; to point an accusing finger and express my anger, pain and loss. I look for something outside of myself to make responsible for the pain I feel inside.

But does blame heal the pain? Does it fix brokenness? Does it restore the loss; does it replace the happiness or joy, now shattered against the oak tree of today's reality? We all know it doesn't. When we ask what is accomplished by determining whose fault led to our pain, we discover that the blame neither heals nor brings resolution to the conflict.

Lemuel taught David how to edit his emotional memory. When Parez broke his truck, David felt pain and anger. He could store that memory of blame and accusation and stay angry or he could replace it with a new picture of forgiveness. Once he let go of the anger and blame, he was able to move ahead and gradually get over the bad thing that had happened to him.

> *"If you cannot free people from their wrongs and see them as the needy people they are, you enslave yourself to your own painful past, and by fastening yourself to the past, you let your hate become your future.*
>
> *For the truth about those who hurt us is that they are weak, needy and fallible human beings . . ."*
> Lewis Smedes, *Forgive and Forget*

The spear of blame and accusation is tied to the pain of the past. Blame keeps you anchored to the loss and pain you felt when you were hurt. It ties you to your own painful history. You cannot move forward if you are tied to the past.

In order to blame someone, you have to emotionally face toward the person in your past that hurt you. Blame requires us to remember and review our hurt. We have to keep the past event current in our memory in order to feel the emotion of anger and blame. Each time we embrace the memory of that pain, it is renewed and reinforced in our minds.

As long as David blames Parez for breaking his truck, he feels anger. He sees Parez through the eyes of judgment. Everything Parez does will be filtered through the pain David attaches to the memory of his broken truck.

The door to future friendship will be closed by unresolved anger from the past.

King David once wrote a song about how God applies the principle of moving west, away from our sins:

> *"As high as the heavens are above the earth, so great is His love for those who fear Him; as far as the east is from the west, so far He has removed our transgressions from us."*
> Psalms 103:11, 12

God takes our sin, sets it behind him to the east, and walks west. Because He's walking away from it, He doesn't see it any more.

David tells us that God's willingness to turn west and walk away from our sins shows God's love for us. It is a right relationship—the power of love—that motivates the heart to turn west and leave our painful past behind. Because He loves us, God wants to forgive even when we hurt His feelings. David writes:

"As a father has compassion on his children, so the Lord has compassion on those who fear Him...
"He does not treat us like our sins deserve or repay us according to our iniquities."
Psalm 103:13, 10.

Because God loves me, He takes the bad things I have done, even if they hurt Him, and puts them behind Him and forgets them forever. Then He comes over and walks beside me into the future as a friend, forgetting what is behind. This is forgiveness.

"I will forgive their wickedness and will remember their sins no more."
Hebrews 8:12

Jesus emphasized the importance of forgiveness to healthy relationships when He taught His disciples to pray. He said they should pray that God would "forgive us our sins as we forgive those who sin against us." (Matthew 6:14, 15).

Perhaps the reason why God cannot forgive my transgressions unless I first forgive those who hurt and wrong me is that, if I chain myself to anger and blame, it is impossible for me to move forward and walk in His forgiveness.

Righteousness requires right relationships. If I will not forgive the person who wrongs me, my relationship to that person is permanently damaged. By choosing anger and blame, I choose to stay chained to the past instead of turning west, as Lemuel said, and moving into the future.

But just knowing the importance of forgiveness to life in God's spiritual kingdom doesn't make it easy to forgive—it only makes it important. How do we find the power to forgive the person who causes us pain? And once we find that strength, how do we let go and leave the wrong we suffered behind?

In the Bible, we read about a concept called 'repentance.' The word means to "change one's mind." It means to change the way I think and believe about my behavior, thoughts and emotions—it literally changes the video playing in our head.

The reason is that when I change the way I think about a behavior, thought or emotion, I automatically begin to change the way I act, think and feel about it.

That's also what happens with forgiveness.

When I change the picture of the event stored in my memory, I automatically change the way I feel and respond to the person and event.

By turning away from the memory of my pain and anger and moving in the opposite direction, I place more distance between myself and the pain that I am leaving behind.

Remember how Joseph's brothers grew jealous of him and sold him to a band of merchants going to Egypt. Joseph had every reason to be angry and bitter. But he chose a different path. He put the wrong and pain he had suffered behind him and built a new, successful life in Egypt.

As a result of forgiveness, he was able to restore his family and provide for them when the famine came.

In the spiritual exercises below, we begin to work on practical ways of reaching forgiveness. And, in the next chapter we will learn new skills for overcoming anger and bitterness.

SPIRITUAL EXERCISE

Several years ago I was speaking at a youth camp in North Dakota. The conference ended on Sunday afternoon but we stayed behind for the night to speak at a church in town. That evening I was walking around the campground when I suddenly fell down a small embankment that was wet from the rain.

So there I was in my Sunday suit, covered with mud! Now I had two choices: either I could throw the suit away and complain about my misfortune, or I could take the suit to the cleaners and have it cleaned so I could use it again.

The logic that compels us to have the suit cleaned appears so obvious that we would question the sanity of anyone who failed to take that option.

You must make the same choices when you are polluted inside by anger or blame after another person wrongs you. If we do not "go to the cleaners" and resolve the pain, we will be stuck with the emotional injury forever.

Spiritual Exercise, Part I: Forgive Yourself.

Each of us fails sometimes. We have all done things we should not have done and not done things we should have done.

This exercise is aimed at recognizing that we need to forgive ourselves. If we do not forgive ourselves, if we do not actually accept God's forgiveness, we will have trouble forgiving others.

First, spend a few minutes talking to God. Tell him you are ready to go to the cleaners and have your heart and soul cleaned. Ask Him to help you see the contents of your own heart and mind during this exercise.

After you have prayed, make the following three lists. (Keep talking to God about what you are thinking as you go through this exercise.)

List One: On the left side of the page, list all of the ways you feel you have failed in your life. List the things you know you should have done but didn't and the things you know you shouldn't have done but you did.

Your goal is to let God clean your heart. It is important that you are honest with Him. Give Him access to the dirt so He can clean it out.

List Two: On a second page, list all of the people whom you believe have been hurt by your words, actions or inactions— whether your intentions were good or not. Don't consider whether your actions were justified; simply list everyone you hurt in the past.
List One may help jog your memory.

Ask God to bring to your mind the names and faces of other people who may have been hurt by anything you have said or done.

List Three: Finally, prepare a third list of all the things you have done which were not what God would have wanted you to do—things that violated His standards of conduct. Many things on this list may be things that no one else knows about except you.

The point is that God already knows. If you act in a way that violates God's instructions, forgiveness is necessary and available.

This exercise may feel too negative at first—but it's not. It may be painful to remember some of these things, but we're here to heal the wounds they have caused you. Remember, we can't get that dirty Sunday suit cleaned until we find where the dirty spot is.

Spiritual Exercise, Part II:

We have just finished identifying areas in your own heart that need to be forgiven. Now we need to apply God's cleaning solution. Remember that forgiveness involves changing the video that runs through our head—editing the memory of the events listed on your three lists to record the act of forgiveness. *"It is the editing of our memory that is our salvation,"* as Lewis Smedes writes.

First, begin to read list One. Ask yourself what emotions you feel when you consider each of the hurts you have caused to another person. Do you regret what you did? If you could go back and do it over again, would you speak or act differently? Knowing that you hurt that person, how do you feel about the pain you have caused?

When you begin to access your feelings about the actions on your list, discuss those feelings with God. Tell him how you feel. Admit that many of the things you said and did hurt other people and that you now realize that you caused pain in their lives.

Now, do the same with Lists Two and Three. Take the time to do this slowly so you can talk each item over with God.

Jesus once said, "Do not judge and you will not be judged. Do not condemn and you will not be condemned. Forgive and you will be forgiven." (Luke 6:37).

This truth applies not just to judging other but also to judging yourself.

If you refuse to forgive yourself for words and actions which have hurt others, you kick God out of His job and become your own judge.

That's not your responsibility. It is God's job to judge. That's why Jesus tells us not to try to do it ourselves.

If I am to be forgiven, I must forgive myself. God wants to forgive me but all to often I stand in the way declaring that I am guilty—condemning myself. We must let God forgive us in order for it to happen.

Take your three lists and admit your sins to God.

Now, accept His willingness to forgive those sins completely. He wants to put them behind you as far as the east is from the west. When He sent His son, Jesus, to pay the legal penalty for our sins, it was because He wanted to forgive us. Now is the time to let Him.

The process of forgiving others and ourselves is just that—a process. Continue to pray and consider the content of your three lists until you feel peace in your heart knowing that you are completely free from those past failures. You have been forgiven. Keep working on the stains until the garment is clean.

The first step to forgiving others is to learn how to forgive ourselves. God is there to help you, because He's trying to do the same thing.

CHAPTER NINE

DIGGING FOR THE ROOT

---

*"In a world full of fugitives,
the person who runs the other direction
is perceived as a madman."*
T.S. Elliot

Parez was nervous about going back to visit David after he had broken his truck. He told David he was sorry about driving his truck into the oak tree. David remembered what Lemuel had said, so he told Parez that it was all behind him now. It was just like old times. They spent the afternoon playing in the pasture and swimming in the pond.

Then Parez had an idea. "Let's take your new .22 to the sand pit and shoot cans," he suggested.

"We can't," David answered. "Esron went to town today, and I can't use the gun unless he's with me."

"He won't know," Parez whispered. "Just take the gun out of the back door when Lemuel isn't looking."

"No. I told Esron I wouldn't use the gun without him, and I won't," David said.

It made Parez mad that David wouldn't cooperate. "We're not going to get in trouble," he argued. "We'll be careful and no one will ever know. Don't be such a chicken."

"No!" said David.

"If you were my friend you wouldn't be so selfish!" Parez yelled. "All you care about is yourself." Parez ran into the house and called his parents to come get him. He wouldn't even talk to David for the rest of the afternoon.

David felt hurt and frustrated. He tried to do what was right, but it ended up wrong. Parez didn't understand. He just got mad instead.

"I don't understand why Parez got mad at me," David told Lemuel. "He knew I was right. Doesn't God like it when we do the right thing?"

"That's a good question," Lemuel responded. "Why do things go wrong when we do what is right?"

Esron got home at about 6:00 o'clock and the first thing he heard was about David and Parez. "You did the right thing," Esron said. "It's dangerous to use the gun without an adult. Someone could get hurt."

"Many years ago, when I was ten years old, just like you, one of the boys on a ranch east of here was killed when the two boys took a gun and went into the woods alone to practice. I felt sad that my friend died. He shouldn't have been killed. If he had listened to his parents, he would have been okay. I'm proud of what you did today," Esron said.

"But I still don't understand why Parez got mad," David said. "How can he be so angry just because he didn't get his way? I feel like I was punished for being good."

"It feels that way sometimes, doesn't it?" Esron agreed. "Tomorrow I have a project that might help you understand Parez a little better. We'll talk about it some more then."

Now David was curious. As he lay down ready to go to sleep, his mind raced back and forth over what had happened that day. Part of him felt good that he had done the right thing and part of him felt sad that Parez had gotten mad anyway.

"I wonder what Esron has planned for tomorrow," he thought to himself.

When David came down for breakfast, he noticed that Esron had pulled the old John Deere tractor up to the back door.

"What's the tractor out there for?" David asked.

"It's time to grub out that old Hickory stump in the backyard," Esron answered. "You better eat a good breakfast. We've got work to do."

After breakfast, they all went to work on the stump. David took the spade and started to dig away the topsoil.

"This isn't so hard," David said after scooping away a little of the black topsoil from around the stump. But just then, he heard a loud "clank" as his shovel hit a rock. He moved his shovel over a few inches and tried again—"clank" it went against the rock again.

"Hey, there's a big rock here," David said. "I don't like the rocks. They make it hard to dig."

"Those rocks remind me of the question you asked me yesterday about Parez," Lemuel piped in.

"Yeah, I should have thrown one at him," David laughed.

"When a person gets mad at you, like Parez did, it may be because of hard places—like a rock—that have formed in their heart where they were hurt before."

"What makes someone get hard places in their heart?" David asked.

"I think it's kind of like the process an oyster uses to make a pearl," Lemuel explained.

"What does that mean?"

"A pearl is formed when a small grain of sand gets stuck inside of the oyster's shell," Lemuel explained. "The grain of sand irritates the oyster and makes a sore spot like a rock in your shoe would. To protect itself, the oyster coats the grain of sand with a hard, smooth coating. But the irritation is still there, so the oyster coats it over and over again until it turns into a big pearl.

"The pearl is like a stone stuck inside of the oyster's shell. Anger and hurt do the same thing to some people if it is left inside of them. It's like that grain of sand. To avoid the irritation we coat the pain with a hard emotional shell. It still bothers us though, so we keep covering it with more and more layers. Pretty soon we have a big hard spot in our hearts where we were hurt in the past."

"Do you think Parez got mad at me because he'd been hurt before, Grandma?" David asked.

"Probably," Lemuel answered. "When someone gets angry because his feelings are hurt, it usually means he has been hurt before and you have accidently poked one of those sore spots in his heart. He feels the old pain again and his anger comes back."

As David and Esron continued to dig around the old hickory stump, they hit one rock after another.

"It's a lot of work getting these rocks out of the ground," David said. "Is it hard to get rocks out of your heart too?"

"It sure is," Lemuel answered. "The longer we let the hard places stay in our heart the bigger they get and the deeper they get buried. Pretty soon we don't even notice that they are there. And if we decide to dig one of those rocks out, we have to move a lot more dirt to get to it."

"How do I keep my heart from getting rocky?" David asked.

"You ask good question," Lemuel said with a smile. "The Bible suggests that we get over being angry right away, it says that we should never let the day end while we are still angry.

David laughed. "Well then, I guess Parez is going to be up pretty late!" he said.

Lemuel smiled and David gave her a big hug. "Remember what we said after Parez broke your truck?" she asked. "Well, that is what it means to not go to bed until you have taken care of the pain that caused you to feel angry that day. King David said it this way in one of his songs:

> *"In your anger do not sin; when you are on your bed search your heart and be silent . . . trust in the Lord."*
>
> Psalm 4:4

"King David knew that if he went to sleep with pain and anger fresh in his heart, he would wake up with a new hard place in his soul. So he practiced replacing pain with trust in God.

"So, if I don't want to have rocks in my heart, I need to put the things that hurt me to the east of me and start moving west before I go to sleep? Is that what you mean?" David asked.

"Exactly. Sometimes it is really hard to forgive what people do to you, but if you don't, you end up making your own heart hard. Jesus said that if your heart is like stony ground, His life will not be able to grow in you for very long."

"I don't want to have hard places in my heart," David said. "I want to keep the stones out of my life."

"When someone gets angry, close your eyes and picture this big hickory stump surrounded by all those rocks. Remember that the roots of that person's heart are surrounded by hard places where they have been hurt before. Let me remind you to search your own heart and learn to trust God so your heart won't get those hard spots in it."

APPLYING THE LESSON

Alertness is a shield against the risk of sin. Peter writes:

> *"Awake! Be on the alert! Your enemy the devil, like a roaring lion, prowls around looking for someone to devour."*
>
> I Peter 5:8

When pain stabs at the heart, it should alert us to the dangers of anger and blame. If we do not quickly identify anger that comes from self-interest when we feel wounded, we will begin to blame and condemn those whom we see as the source of our pain. The Bible tells us that unresolved anger will, by the next morning, begin to create hard spots in our heart.

If I cut my finger, the cut provides and opportunity for infection and germs to enter my body. When a finger is cut, the first thing a mother will do is to wash the wound and apply a disinfectant. Then she will cover the wound with a protective bandage to keep the germs out. If the cut doesn't heal right away, she cleans it again each day to prevent infection.

Feelings of anger are cuts to our emotional flesh. They must be treated in much the same way to prevent infection in our souls. When we are wronged, it wounds our heart. When I feel emotional pain, my heart is vulnerable to the intrusion of the infecting elements of anger, bitterness, judgment and selfishness.

Pain produces a natural inclination to withdraw from its source and as a result, we often pull away from relationships when we are hurt and sometimes we use anger to create that distance. If anger is allowed to infect us, bitterness soon sets in. A desire for revenge and judgment begins to grow in our heart like a stone. When these emotions bear fruit, we start to act in ways that contradict God's pattern for healthy relationships.

So how do we keep our hearts pure when we feel hurt? How do we clean the emotional wounds and deal with anger before it gets lodged in our heart? How do we keep the stone from forming around our wound?

First, remember the stony dirt around the old hickory stump behind Lemuel's house. Recognize the danger of not dealing with anger quickly before the rocks form. Stay alert, like Peter instructed, so that you can deal with your anger quickly.

A friend of mine named Janice and her husband had filed for divorce. She came to my office seeking advice. They had been married for fifteen years, and she did not want the marriage to end. However, she had mixed feelings about her present situation because there were things that her husband Dave did that she didn't like.

As we talked, Janice shared several things that Dave had done over the years that wounded her. As she recalled incident after incident, I was impressed at how clear her memory was of these past hurts. Many of the offenses she shared were small things, but they hurt her just the same.

I finally asked her how she could remember so much detail years after all of these things had happened. Janice told me how she had kept a calendar in the kitchen where she would write down what happened each time Dave did or said something that hurt her feelings. She didn't want him to be able to deny them later.

Jesus told his disciples a parable about stony ground. He explained that stony ground prevents the roots of a relationship with God from taking hold. The plant cannot grow deep enough roots to survive because of the rocks, which lie below the surface of the topsoil.

It's the same with earthly relationships. When the heart's soil had been hardened by anger or bitterness;

the roots of love, patience, kindness and forgiveness have no place to grow. Even though relationships may spring up quickly, like the plants in Jesus' story, they do not last because there is no room in the heart for a healthy root system.

Janice came back to visit for several weeks to talk about her marriage. She shared how her anger had grown year after year as she kept track of every hurt. She felt herself slowly growing hard and cold toward her husband in order to protect herself from the next potential wound. Now Dave was threatening to leave her because she was angry all of the time. Janice had let her heart become like stony ground where there was no room for love to build a healthy root system.

When Paul said we should never let the sun go down on our anger, he wasn't suggesting that we be doormats or sissies. He was telling us how to keep our own hearts clear of the stones, which infect the heart and make it hard. A pure heart is stronger than a wounded heart. Clean soil is more productive than stony ground.

Because she had stored anger in her heart for so long, Janice no longer could accept or respect her husband. She was destroying her marriage with the residual effects of anger she felt from minor events that had happened years ago.

What is the solution?

Deal quickly with the pain that fresh wounds cause us quickly—before anger can take root and begin to harden within us. Pain and anger are natural responses when we feel hurt. We must learn how to use forgiveness and love to clean and heal new wounds quickly.

Being honest with ourselves is an important ingredient to cleaning fresh wounds. Admit that you are hurt. Don't hide it from God. Talk to Him about it.

Healing comes when we let go of the pain. Forgiveness and time spent with God are critical to that process. Depending on how you were hurt, it may take some time for a wound to heal—but it is important to cleanse the wound and start immediately.

Anger not only divides relationships; it often hides the role we may have played in the event we are angry about. Anger is a blame reaction. God tells us to examine ourselves and to admit our own sin quickly. If something you did made the painful situation worse, admit it to God and accept His forgiveness up front.

In addition, Paul teaches us to, "Be patient in affliction . . . bless those who persecute you . . . Do not repay evil for evil . . . Do not take revenge." (Romans 12:12-14). That's a lot to ask! Why is this so important that God put it in the Bible?

It is because before you can avenge a wrong you have suffered, you have to judge the one who wronged you. You have to find them guilty of an offense for which they need to be punished.

The spiritual problem is that the other person is also a child of God whom He wants to forgive and restore—not punish. He already had His Son pay for the wrong that they did to you when He paid the penalty for their sins on the cross. That means that when I judge them guilty and in need of punishment and revenge, I am disagreeing with God. You cannot both avenge and forgive the same wrong—those two attitudes are exclusive.

The process of erasing hurt and cleansing fresh wounds takes time, prayer and intention. It's not easy but it is important. It's more important to you than it is to the one who hurt you because of the risk of infection that comes from being wounded.

Healing requires that we give up the right to get even—that we choose to release the wrongdoer from the consequences of our anger and that we place the wrong behind us as we walk forward toward God each day. If we do that, the hurt will be farther behind us each day because we have decided not to take it with us on life's journey.

SPIRITUAL EXERCISE

The carnal nature we were born with tells us we should get even when we are hurt. When we learn to release our anger and forgive, we break that cycle of violence.

> *"Forgiving is a miracle, however, that few of us have the magic to perform easily."*
> Louis Smede, *Forgive and Forget*

The longer you hold pain in the soul, the thicker and harder its protective covering grows. Unresolved pain grows in weight and effect over time. The longer I fail to forgive, the harder it becomes. Eventually, we grow accustomed to the pain as if it were normal. As a result, the stones begin to accumulate in the soul.

Several years ago, when my daughters were small, we decided to have a family garage sale. Each person selected several things to contribute to the sale. Each of the girls chose some toys they no longer needed from the toy box.

But when the day came to put everything out on the driveway to sell, they wanted to hang on to their toys and take them back in the house.

At first I tried logic: "No, you already have plenty of other toys in the house." But they pleaded to keep their toys. A compromise was reached when they each were given $10 that they could use to shop at the garage sale and buy back what was most important to them.

In much the same way we sometimes tend to buy back the pain and anger of the past after we feel we have forgiven it. We pray a quick prayer of forgiveness but a few days later, the old feelings begin to return.

In this exercise, we will work to dig out some of the hard stones of anger that may be hiding in our soul from past hurts. Just like it took David a long time to dig the stones out from around the old hickory stump, this process will take time and effort.

Spiritual Exercise, Part I: List below the names of the three people who have hurt you the most deeply:

1. _____

2. _____

3. _____

Now recall all of the specific acts that each of these people did which you feel caused you to be hurt. (You can use a separate piece of paper if you need more room to write your list.)

1. Name: _____

2. Name: _____

3. Name: _____

Finally, list below all of the ways that the wrongs these people committed against you have limited, injured or hurt you.

1. Name: _____

2. Name: _____

3. Name: _____

You have just defined the three biggest rocks in the soil of your soul. Now our job is to get them out.

Spiritual Exercise, Part II:

David had to move a lot of dirt in order to pry the big rocks away from the stump. Surgery is painful and invasive, but we are better off and healthier afterward.

Now we go to the last part of this exercise: meditation. To meditate means to visualize in our minds a reality that we have not or cannot hold in our hands. It means to program and reprogram the video of our memories by using our thought process and imagination. By the process of Godly meditation, we alter our memory of past events by seeing a new meaning in what happened before.

First, picture in your mind the person who hurt you. Make the picture full size so it fills the screen of your mind. Look at the things they did and said that hurt you. Now, look past them and see the picture of Jesus hanging on the cross, dying for the sins they committed against you.

Zoom in on Jesus so you can see and hear what He is saying. Listen as He says to the soldier pounding a big nail into His hands to kill Him, "Father, forgive them." Watch as He carries the forgiveness of your sins and theirs with Him as he suffers.

Now take the list of wrongs that this person did that hurt you and carry it with you over to that cross. Put it there at the foot of the cross, right next to the list of sins you have committed that he paid for that day. Listen as He says, "Father, forgive them both. It is finished."

Pray this prayer:

"Jesus, I realize that ___(name)___ was forgiven for what he did to hurt me on the day you died. It was finished that day. Please give me the strength to let the pain and anger I feel go. Give me the strength to live under the umbrella of Your forgiveness."

Now, repeat this meditation for each of the three people on your list. If the stones are old and buried deep inside of you, you may need to revisit this exercise several times to finish the process of forgiveness.

> *"In pure love, which is completely detached and abandoned, the soul feeds itself in silence on the cross and on its union with Jesus Christ crucified, without any reversion to its own suffering."*
>
> François Fenelon

Spend enough time with Jesus to learn to forgive the way He does.

CHAPTER TEN

THE POWER OF LETTING GO

---

*"Do not be overcome with evil,
but overcome evil with good."*
Romans 12:21

I t took all morning for David and Esron to dig the rocks away from the old hickory stump. Lemuel fixed a big lunch for the work crew and they sat on the back porch and admired their work.

"Well, I think we're just about ready to hook the chain around the stump and pull it out with the tractor," Esron noted.

"Wait. I want another brownie first!" David said.

After lunch, Esron and David wrapped the big old log chain around the stump twice. David took the other end of the chain and hooked onto the back of the tractor.

"Stand over by Lemuel so you don't get hit by anything," Esron said.

David ran over to the porch and grabbed another brownie as Esron put the tractor into gear and started to move slowly forward. The chain pulled tight and the engine throttled down as it began to pull at the stump. The right tire slipped in the dirt and then, suddenly, the chain snapped and the tractor bounced forward. The broken chain flew up and almost hit Esron.

"Are you alright?" Lemuel asked.

"Yes, I'm fine," Esron answered. "That old stump is a lot more stubborn than I thought. I guess we will have to dig deeper around the roots before we can pull it out."

So David and Esron spent the afternoon digging deeper and deeper into the ground around the stump.

"This is too much work," David said. "Let's finish it some other day."

"No, we need to finish what we started," Esron replied. "We have all of the tools out now, and if we don't finish the job, it will sit here like this and never get done."

"If we don't get the stump out now, we will only end up with a bigger mess later," Lemuel added. "It's like the problem we talked about yesterday where the oyster keeps putting hard layers around the spot that irritates it. Anger that is left in the heart for too long grows roots that go deeper and deeper into our soul. When anger grows deep roots, it is called bitterness."

"This stump has been here for a long time," David insisted. "It's not going anywhere."

Esron and David got the shovels and started digging even deeper into the ground around the stump.

"Are we going to get to China pretty soon," David asked with a smile.

Esron took an old axe and began to chop off the big roots about two feet below the surface. When the hole was about thirty inches deep around the stump, Esron's axe hit a rock with a big clank.

"I guess we're going to have to dig some more rocks out before we chop off the rest of roots," Esron observed.

"I'll get the rock out while you sharpen the axe," David said boldly.

He climbed down in the hole and began to dig around the rock. But he couldn't find the edge of it. He went to the other side of the root and the rock was over there too.

"You're going to have to come help me with this one, Grandpa," David said. "It's too big for me to get out."

Esron got down in the hole and helped David dig around the rock. Finally, he stood up and said, "Well, look at this Grandpa. The roots of the old stump have wrapped themselves completely around this rock like an anchor. No wonder it wouldn't come out the first time."

They dug all the way around the rock and found that the roots had wrapped themselves around the big stone like the arms of a child afraid of a monster in the night.

"We're going to need to cut off all of the roots to get this stump out," Esron concluded.

"This is the most stubborn stump I've ever seen," David said. "It won't let go."

"Sounds to me a lot like your Aunt Irene!" Lemuel laughed.

"What does she have to do with it?" David asked. "And why does she always seem as if she is mad at something when she comes to visit?"

"That's what I mean," Lemuel explained. "Many years ago her husband Caleb left her for another woman. She was hurt and angry for a long time. But she never learned how to forgive and get the stone of anger out of her heart. So the rest of her life grew around that big stone like the roots of that stump. She just couldn't let it go. She let the roots of bitterness anchor the pain of the past in her heart."

"If it happened a long time ago, why is she still mad?" David asked.

"Because she's still hanging on to the pain she felt when Caleb left her. She's connected to it like those roots that are wrapped around that big stone. She never dug down and cut off the roots so she could get rid of her anger."

"I don't understand why she would rather be mad?" David said. "Doesn't it get boring after a while?"

"I don't think she really wants to be mad any more, David. But she did not learn how to forgive and let God heal her heart, so the stone just stayed there and got bigger. Then the rest of her life just grew in around it like those roots around the rock."

"Is that what will happen to Parez if he doesn't learn how to stop being mad?"

"It can happen to any of us who keep the stones of anger in our hearts instead of letting God dig them out for us. The rest of our lives begin to gradually grow around that anger and it gets harder and harder to get over."

"Well, it's sure a lot of work getting this stump out after the roots go around the big stone," David said.

"You're right," Lemuel answered. "That's why God tells us not to let the roots of bitterness grow in our hearts. If we don't ever let those roots start to grow around the hard places inside of us, we will never end up like this stubborn old stump.

"As you get older, remember to forgive as quickly as you can. If someone hurts you, remember that your anger hurts you more than it does them. Go talk to God and let him help you heal that pain you feel.

"Remember the picture of the old hickory stump in your mind whenever you need to forgive someone. Give God the axe and let him cut off the roots that connect you to the pain so that you can move on with your life. Don't let anger and pain from the past tie you down to anger of things that happened a long time ago."

APPLYING THE LESSON

Sometimes God's directions for how to solve problems seem backwards from our natural instincts. For example, He says, "Consider it pure joy, my brothers, whenever you face trials of many kinds . . ." (James 1:2). We think, "I'd be happy if I don't have to deal with any problems today!"

It sometimes takes a lifetime to learn that God's way of dealing with adversity, pain and struggle actually works better than our own methods.

Irene was legitimately hurt by the adultery and desertion of her husband. But she made everything worse because she didn't use God's tools for dealing with her pain. Instead she stayed angry and grew bitter, refusing to forgive Caleb for having "ruined her life."

The result of her decision to stay mad and bitter was an unhappy life. She hung on so tightly to her righteous sense of anger that she couldn't reach the goodness, opportunity and blessings that otherwise could have been hers.

If Irene had chosen a different path—a path of forgiveness, restoration and regeneration—she would have had a different life. Bitterness tied her down like the roots of the old hickory stump wrapped around a big boulder.

One of the reasons why God allows us to suffer pain, humiliation and failure is so that we can see our own hearts—we can learn who we are in the midst of adversity. If we choose blame and anger, we blind ourselves to what God can teach us because we are only looking at what the other person did. That means we may have to face the same adversity all over again to try to learn the lesson we missed the first time.

God's purpose is to get us in a right relationship with Him. We naturally try to defend and justify ourselves, but God wants us to admit our weaknesses and learn the power of humility.

The fact that someone violated one of my rights and hurt me is no reason to respond in ways that violate God's purpose and directions for my life.

> *"There is no heaven with a little corner of hell in it. God is determined to make you pure and holy and right. He will not allow you to escape for one moment from the scrutiny of the Holy Spirit. He urged you to come to judgment right away when He convicted you, but you did not; the inevitable process began to work and*

now you are in prison, and you will only get out
when you have paid the uttermost farthing."
Oswald Chambers

James explains why God allows us to face adversity. "You know that the testing of your faith develops perseverance. Perseverance must finish its work so that you may be mature and complete, not lacking anything." (James 1:3, 4). Like the sculptor's chisel on a piece of granite, adversity is God's way of completing the development of our spiritual character.

Jesus was tested and faced adversity, just like we do.

"I want you to know Christ . . . and the
fellowship of sharing in his sufferings, becoming
like him in his death."
Philippians 3:10.

Difficult circumstances can help us become stronger if we respond to them correctly. Just as physical exercise is designed to challenge the muscles in our body, so adversity exercises our character and spirituality.

"God is ingenious in making his crosses. He
makes them of iron and lead, which are heavy in
themselves.

He makes them of straw which seems to
weigh nothing, and which is no less difficult to
carry.

He makes them of gold and precious stones,

*which dazzle the spectators, which excite the
envy of the public, but which crucify no less than
the crosses which are most despised.*

*He makes them of all the things which we like
the best, and turns them to bitterness."*

Francois Fenelon, *Christian Perfection*

It is difficult to let go of blame when I am hurt and
angry. But blame prevents me from taking responsibility for the difficult work of mercy, forgiveness
and self-examination. My resentment now begins to
define who I am.

God tells us to "get rid of all bitterness, rage and
anger . . . along with every form of malice." We are
told how to do this: "forgive each other, just as in
Christ, God forgave you." Ephesians 4:31,32.

How do you know if bitterness has taken root in
your heart? Watch for symptoms of defensiveness,
blame or secret anger. When you find yourself being
defensive or blaming when you are challenged, it may
be a symptom that you have a root of blame and anger
in your heart. If you feel a lot more anger inside than
other people realize, then you have found a root that
needs to be cut of and removed to set your heart free
to reach the positive good God has for you.

Now it is time to get out the shovel of God's Word
and the axe of His spiritual presence and start digging.

SPIRITUAL EXERCISE

Bitterness is a petrified resentment that anchors the
soul to the past. It locks the soul in a cycle of blame
and anger that prevents the heart from seeing its own

sins or from accepting the good that is available to it. The Bible is clear about this principle:

> *"You, therefore, have no excuse, you who pass judgment on someone else, for at whatever point you judge the other, you are condemning yourself, because you who pass judgment do the same things."*
>
> Romans 2:1

What are the consequences of bitterness? King Saul is an example. He became bitter that God had chosen David to be the next king instead of one of his own sons. He was defensive about his feelings and critical of David—he became a blamer. He blamed everyone but himself and stuffed his anger inside until it threatened to explode in a violent rage.

After a few years, his bitterness consumed him. He began to become ill emotionally and psychologically. He ended up in spiritual bondage and deception and ultimately committed suicide. Why? Because he let his bitterness own him instead of digging out the root and letting his resentment go. His entire life was changed the day he welcomed resentment into his heart. The root of bitterness often lies hidden deep in the heart where we don't notice it from the surface. But it still anchors us to a negative past.

Spiritual Exercise, Part I: Get your Bible and read the story of King Saul in I Samuel. You'll find it in Chapters 9-19 and Chapters 28 and 31. Take a notebook or piece of paper and write down each of the emotions that Saul uses in response to events in his life.

Make a list of the things that made Saul feel angry. Make a second list of each time he blamed someone else for a problem he was facing. Notice the trail of his emotional decline and notice how it follows the track of his anger and blame.

Now do the same exercise on a personal basis. Select the one person whom you would least like to see and spend time with or give a hug to right now. Write down why you don't like that person. What has that person done that hurt you or made you dislike them?

Focus on your emotions as you think about this person. How do you feel? How have they made you feel in the past? Do you see any similar emotions to those experienced by Saul? Dig down inside and see if you find any stones of resentment hidden there within your heart.

Now think about God's commands to show mercy, forgive others and to love each other as we love ourselves. What anger and resentment reveal to us is our own need for God—when we hang on to these feelings like Saul did, we are violating God's laws.

There is nothing you can do to change what happened to you. But you have complete control over how you react to it and how you let that event change your life.

Spiritual Exercise, Part II: Now, we need to move past the recognition of bitterness or resentment in our hearts and deal with our own inner cleansing. We need to find the roots and cut them off; one at a time, like Esron removing a stump.

First, think about the hurts you have identified from your past and thank God for allowing you to suffer in ways that make your heart sensitive to your need for Him. "Give thanks in all circumstances, for this is God's will for you in Christ Jesus." (I Thessalonians 5:17).

Being grateful in the face of suffering requires strength of spirit and character. Paul responded to adversity by saying, "Though outwardly we are wasting away, yet inwardly we are being renewed day by day. For our light and momentary troubles are achieving for us an eternal glory that far outweighs them all." (II Corinthians 4:16,17). Notice that the inward was not controlled by outward circumstances.

Now list on a separate piece of paper all of the ways that problems, adversity and struggle have helped you to become a stronger person. Did it help you to become more resourceful? What new things did you learn from these struggles? Did it help you to become more forgiving? Did it allow you to understand other people better? Did it prepare you for new challenges?

Second, list all the ways your past hurts have helped you to see your own heart and emotions. Now take time to thank God for all of the positive things you have gained from the negative experiences in your life.

Finally, you must cut off the root of blame. As long as you blame the ones who hurt you, there will be an emotional anchor holding you to the past. The axe God gives us to cut of the roots of blame within us is mercy.

Mercy means to look at someone who is guilty, someone who has hurt or wronged us, someone whom we have a legitimate right to condemn and forgive him of his guilt toward us. *"Do not be overcome by evil, but overcome evil with good."* Romans 12:21. This is the power of mercy.

The power of mercy is strong enough to overcome the evil of bitterness and anger, which binds our hearts to past wounds.

Copy the following prayer onto a small card and pray it each day until it reflects how you really feel.

> *"Father, I was wronged and hurt by what _____ did to me. I have blamed him for the pain and suffering that I have experienced as a result of what he did. I am here now to tell you that I no longer blame him or bring any accusation against him before You. I have forgiven him, and I want You to forgive him of what he did to me as well. I release him from any consequences of his sin against me, and I ask You to embrace him fully with your love and grace."*

CHAPTER ELEVEN

NO PROBLEM TOO SMALL

---

*"You have withered your heart by so eagerly
pursuing your own wishes regardless of God's will.
This is the cause of all you are suffering."*
Fenelon, *The Royal Way of the Cross*

Every day at 11:00 o'clock, David and Lemuel would walk up the long gravel driveway to the mailbox to see what the mailman had brought that day. And each day, Lemuel told David a story of how God had worked in her life.

"Grandma, you walk slow," David teased, as he ran on down the road ahead of her. He walked over and sat on the white wooden fence until she caught up to him. "You must be running out of gas. It seems like you walk slower every day!"

"I do feel like I'm low on fuel today," Lemuel answered. "Wait until you are eighty years old and see how frisky you are!" She didn't tell him about her cancer. She didn't want him to worry.

David skipped along the road and picked a bouquet of wild daisies.

"Here, Grandma," he said, "I picked some flowers for you. It's fun staying here with you and Grandpa."

He darted down the road and then stopped suddenly. Lemuel could tell something was wrong. David was twisting and shaking his ankle like it hurt.

"What's wrong?" Lemuel asked as she caught up to him.

"Something's wrong with my foot," David said, limping over to Lemuel. "It feels like there's a nail in my shoe. It hurts every time I step on it."

"Step down on it and tell me where it hurts," Lemuel suggested.

David limped across the road and then back to Lemuel.

"It hurts right by my heel," David said. "There's a nail in my shoe."

"I don't think it's a nail. Those are tennis shoes," Lemuel answered with a smile. "Come over here; take off your shoe and let me see what's wrong."

David sat down, untied his shoe and handed it to Lemuel.

"Well, here's your problem," Lemuel said. "You have a piece of sand in your shoe."

"A piece of sand!" David exclaimed. "There must be more than a piece of sand. It really hurt."

"It only takes a little stone to hurt your foot," Lemuel answered.

"But how could one grain of sand hurt so much?" He asked.

"God made us that way to protect us," Lemuel replied. "He made an early warning system in our bodies to warn us when we are in danger of being hurt. That grain of sand hurts you so that you will stop and get it out of your shoe before it gets worse. If you don't, it will irritate your foot and get more painful until your foot gets infected and you can't walk on it at all."

"It doesn't seem like one little grain of sand should hurt so much," David said as he put his shoe back on.

"If it didn't hurt that much, you wouldn't have stopped to fix it," Lemuel replied. "God does the same thing in the rest of our lives too," she added. "Do you remember the other night when you touched the skillet with the chicken frying in it?"

"That hurt too," David replied. "I got my hand out of there in a hurry! Look, I still have a red spot on my finger."

"Well, that was like the grain of sand in your shoe," Lemuel explained. "God made your fingers sensitive to heat so that you would pull away as soon as you touched it. If you left your hand on the skillet, it would burn you much worse."

"So should I be glad that my foot hurts from one little grain of sand?" David asked.

"Yes, and you should learn to be the same way in your heart," Lemuel explained. "When you are friends with God, it will hurt when you get something in your heart that doesn't belong there."

"The only thing that's going to get in my heart is blood," David laughed.

Lemuel smiled and said, "God calls the secret inner part of us our hearts. If you heart stops working you are physically dead; if your spiritual heart doesn't work, you are spiritually dead. God said He would write His laws in our hearts. That means that if I do something wrong, I will feel pain like you did in your shoe because I broke one of the laws He has put in my heart. It is God's way of telling me to get that grain of sand out of my heart before my heart becomes infected."

"How do I know when there is a grain of sand in my heart?" David asked.

"Unless you pay attention, you might not notice," Lemuel answered. "Remember when we talked about Luke's dog whistle and how God's voice is hard to hear unless we pay attention and learn to recognize what it sounds like?"

"God's voice doesn't seem very loud sometimes," David said.

"That's true," Lemuel answered. "But it was just a small pain that you felt when the grain of sand first got in your shoe, wasn't it?"

"At first I barely noticed it was there, but as I kept walking it started to hurt more and more." David answered.

"That's exactly the way you will feel in your heart if there is something there that shouldn't be," Lemuel said. "First, God's small voice makes us feel just a little uncomfortable. But if we ignore that feeling, the grain of sand in our heart hurts more and more.

"When I was a little girl our family was poor, and I had only one pair of shoes. They were plain, brown high-top shoes. My father would clean and oil them every Saturday night so that they would look good when we went to church on Sunday. But

I always noticed that most of the other girls had special shoes for Sunday. Then on my sixteenth birthday, I received my first pair of high-heeled dress shoes. I was so excited.

"Now I was just like my friends. But the new shoes hurt my feet. They were tight and hard. It seemed as if they pinched my feet every time I took a step. I thought that was the way high heels always felt. So even though my feet hurt, I kept wearing them because I wanted to look good to my friends.

"After a few weeks, my feet had calluses where the shoes pinched me, and I didn't notice that they hurt any more. It was almost a year later that I was in Simpson's Shoe Store trying on new shoes and realized that all high heels didn't hurt my feet the way that first pair had."

"You should have tried a bigger pair right away," David suggested.

"That's right," Lemuel replied. "Because I ignored the message of my sore feet, it took me a long time to learn that what I was doing wasn't good for me. It's the same way when something makes your heart feel uncomfortable. You should get it out of your heart right away. If you ignore the small discomfort in your soul and keep doing what bothers you, calluses will grow on your heart, just like they grew on my feet. And, if you get calluses on your heart, you will no longer be able to hear the voice of God very well."

"What happens if I do take the grains of sand out of my heart when they first start to bother me?" David asked.

"Well . . . How does your foot feel now?" Lemuel asked.

"My foot's fine," David answered. "The sand didn't hurt it."

"That's exactly what happens in your heart too," Lemuel answered. "If you get those things out of your heart when they first make you feel uncomfortable, they will not make your heart hard or calloused like those shoes did my feet. It won't hurt anymore."

APPLYING THE LESSON

Solomon told a story that made this same point. His wrote a story of a love relationship between a king and a simple, poor shepherd girl. In this love story, the King says:

> "Catch us the foxes, the little foxes that ruin
> the vineyards, our vineyards that are in bloom."
> Song of Solomon 2:15

The wise king knew that there would be many little things that could undermine the roots of their relationship if they did not pay attention to them—like baby foxes digging holes around the roots of their grape vines.

As a boy, Solomon had seen how much damage the foxes could do to vines in his father's vineyards. He recognized that the same thing happens to relationships—they can be undermined by small, seemingly insignificant things, like that grain of sand in your shoe. If not eliminated quickly, these small things can kill the vines.

Lemuel used the pain of a single grain of sand in your shoe to illustrate the importance of responding to small sins when they prick the conscience. Although the sin may only produce a small discomfort in the soul, its long-term effect can create permanent damage to our relationship to God—like small foxes ruining the vines in a vineyard. It may start with a small compromise, a little shift in priorities, a surrender to self-interest, but when it grows, it produces deadly results in our hearts.

Still, we often argue, "No one is perfect, and God can't be too upset by such small compromises." The danger of this logic is that it distorts the truth by looking at sin from the perspective of its effect on God rather than viewing it from the perspective of its effect on us. It is not the foxes that suffer when the vines are ruined; it is the vines.

We must remember that sin is sin because it hurts us. God didn't sit down and make a list of do's and don'ts just so we'd have a list of things to obey or disobey. When we read in the Bible that a behavior, emotion or act is wrong, it is because of the harm it causes to others and ourselves. It is the pain and damage that sin causes to the people He loves that makes these things objectionable to God.

Mark, an air force pilot, came up to me after a seminar I was teaching in North Dakota a few years ago. He had been teaching a Sunday school class and had noticed a pretty girl sitting near the back. He smiled at her and she smiled back. He went over to meet her after class.

Mark was married. As he talked to this girl, he felt attracted to her, yet at the same time, he felt a twinge of guilt because he knew he should not be feeling this way. I shared with Mark how the same thing happened to King David when he sat on the roof of the palace and watched Bathsheba, which led to adultery, murder and the death of a child for David. That little fox ruined a big part of his life.

Much like David, Mark knew he should not pursue a friendship with Beth, and he told himself he was just being a friend. But his desire grew because he didn't listen to the voice of his conscience within himself. A few months later, he left his wife and family and moved in with Beth. The relationship didn't last long but it totally ruined Mark's relationship with his wife and children. He wanted to know how to put it all back together again.

Lemuel's lesson could have saved Mark and his family a lot of pain. When he first noticed the small grain of sand in his heart—that first twinge of conscience—it would have been easy to do the right thing and walk away from the desire he had felt. But he didn't. He allowed it to grow until it did what sin always does in the end—it caused destruction. Like little foxes ruining the vines in the vineyard.

It may seem overly religious to be so sensitive about small acts of sin, but remember: small foxes can ruin large vines. And when the vines are dead, your life will produce no crop. Only when sin is small is it easy to catch the fox. The longer you wait the harder it becomes. Lemuel's advice was to stop and clean the grain of sand out of your heart before it becomes infected.

> *"Whenever a man desires anything outside of God's order, he is immediately disquieted within himself."*
> Thomas a Kempis, *The Imitation of Christ*

SPIRITUAL EXERCISE

When I was a child, we had a Golden Retriever named Duke. When everyone was in the house, Duke would sit outside the door with his nose right where the door would open. If anyone opened the door two inches or more, Duke stuck his nose in the door, fighting to get into the house. Peter tells us that sin acts just the same way. It crouches at the door, waiting for the first opportunity to sneak into the soul.

God picks Job as an example of a life well lived. In the middle of the worst disappointment, suffering and loss you could imagine, Job tells us why he still had peace in his heart:

> *"I will maintain my righteousness and never let go of it; my conscience will not reproach me as long as I live."*
>
> Job 27:6

Job practiced what Lemuel taught David. He kept his conscience clear of any offense—he removed every small pebble as soon as he found it.

Spiritual Exercise, Part I: In this exercise, we will begin to record a spiritual history. The Bible tells us there is a cause and effect relationship between choices and behavior. If you record and study your own life history, you will begin to see what works and why things sometimes fail.

Begin with this prayer, *"Father, show me what the effect in my life has been of ignoring the voice of my conscience when I knew that what I was doing was wrong."*

Now think back over your life and describe one incident when you felt the voice of conviction concerning something you were about to do and where you ignored that voice and did it anyway.

Describe the incident: _____

_____

Next, look back at all of the results of that choice. How did it make you feel about yourself? How do you feel when you talk to God about it? How did it affect the other people involved? Was it hard to break the pattern of behavior once you had started it?

Results of my actions: _____

_____

Jesus' brother, James, tells us the long-term results of ignoring our conscience and continuing to do what we know is wrong.

> "Each one is tempted when, by his own evil desire, he is dragged away and enticed. Then, after desire has conceived, it gives birth to sin; and sin, when it is full-grown, gives birth to death."
> James 1:14, 15.

Spiritual Exercise, Part II: In each of our lives, there have been times when we have felt the grain of sand in our heart—the still small voice of conscience—and we have disregarded that voice to our own detriment. Take a few minutes each day for the next week and ask God to take you back to those choices and tell you once again where you wandered from the path so that you can find your way back to the center of His will.

This exercise is about redeveloping our sensitivity to God's small voice. It is about rediscovering the peace that comes from having a clean heart.

Finally, use this prayer of St. Thomas á Kempis as a meditation. Pray it each morning as part of your devotional time. Make it your personal affirmation to God.

"For not every desire proceeds from the Holy Spirit, even though it seems right and good. My son, say this about everything: "Lord, if this is pleasing to you, so let it be. Lord, it is for Your honor, let it be done in Your name. But if you know it will be harmful to me, and hurtful to the health of my soul, take away the desire from me.

"Grant me always to desire and to will what you most accept. Let Your will be mine, and let my will always follow Yours. Grant that I may die to all things that are in the world. Grant to me above all things that can be desired, to rest in You, and in You to have my heart and peace. In this peace, that is, in You, I will sleep and rest. Amen."

Thomas á Kempis, *The Imitation of Christ*

CHAPTER TWELVE

MUDDY SUNDAY

---

*"Through pride we deceive ourselves.
Deep down below the surface of the
conscience, a still small voice
says to us something is out of tune."*
Carl Jung

When David woke up Sunday morning, it was raining again. Sundays were always special. Lemuel would prepare a big breakfast, and they would all get dressed up in their best clothes to go to church. David liked Sundays because he didn't have to help Esron with chores.

David could smell the bacon cooking as he got dressed in his white shirt and khakis. As David came down for breakfast, Esron was just getting in from feeding the animals. He looked as if he had just taken a shower with all of his clothes on.

"You're soaked!" Lemuel said. "Take this cup of coffee and go get cleaned up while I prepare your breakfast."

"I'm ready to eat now," David declared as he sat down at the table.

Lemuel gave him a plate with pancakes, bacon and eggs, along with a glass of freshly squeezed orange juice.

"I'll go check on Esron while you eat," she said. "Be careful not to spill on your white shirt. All of your other good clothes are dirty."

In a few minutes Esron was back for his breakfast. "We really need this rain," he said. "The garden is going to spurt after this."

"And so will the weeds," added David, knowing that he would be the one assigned to weed the garden next week.

"Isn't it interesting how the rain helps both the good and the bad to grow?" Lemuel said. "It's as if God puts his blessing over everything and then sorts it all out later."

"Look, Grandma," David interrupted. "The rain is letting up. Maybe we should go now, before it starts again."

"Comb your hair and get your Bible," Lemuel answered. "I'll clear the table and put the food away while you get ready."

Esron went out to the barn and got the pickup. He drove up in front of the house so that Lemuel and David could keep their feet dry.

"How come you never lock the house?" David asked as they walked out to the truck.

"I've lived out here for eighty years, and no one has ever locked that door," Lemuel answered. "We've always just trusted God to take care of us. I don't think we could find a key if we needed it. Besides, Luke will guard the place while we're gone."

No sooner had Lemuel spoken his name than Luke came running up to say good morning. Luke had been out in the rain and was covered in water and mud.

David saw what was coming. "No, Luke! Stay down!" He yelled as Luke lunged at him to give him a kiss.

It was too late. Luke left muddy paw prints all over David's clean white shirt.

"Oh, no!" David said. "Look at me. These clothes are ruined. What are we going to do Grandma? Luke made a mess of my Sunday clothes."

Lemuel could see the small tears of disappointment starting to gather in David's eyes as he looked at the mess Luke had made of his shirt. Esron turned off the truck as Lemuel put her arm around David and led him back into the house.

"Take those clothes off, and I'll take care of them for you," Lemuel said.

"I don't have anything else to wear to church," David said. "What are we going to do? I hate it when Luke jumps on me like that. Why doesn't he ever pay attention to what I say?"

"Well, remember yesterday when you spent most of the morning outside wrestling with Luke in the yard," Lemuel answered. "I don't think Luke can tell the difference between when you want to play and when you are all dressed up for church."

"I told him to stay down, and he still jumped all over me," David complained.

"Why do you think you are so upset that Luke jumped on you today, when you were asking him to wrestle with you yesterday?" Lemuel asked.

"Yesterday I was just wearing a dirty pair of jeans and an old shirt," David answered. "It didn't matter if he got me dirty or not. Those clothes needed to be washed anyway."

"The way you feel about Luke is the way people feel about sin in their lives," Lemuel observed. "When our hearts are dirty and covered with sin, it doesn't seem to bother us if Satan jumps all over us. But if we let God cleanse us and give us a clean heart, we are upset at even the small sins that get us dirty again," she explained.

"How does God give us a clean heart?" David asked.

"Well, did you notice what I just did with your white shirt to get Luke's paw prints off of it?" Lemuel answered.

"You sprayed it with the spot remover and put it in the washer to rinse," David answered. "But God can't stick me in the washing machine every time I get dirty."

"In a way, that is exactly what He does. If you do something that you know is wrong and get your heart dirty with sin, God says that you should admit to Him that you have gotten dirty and ask Him to forgive you. Then He says He will forgive you and cleanse your heart. He sprays the dirty spots with the power of His forgiveness and then rinses your heart with the presence of His spirit to be sure there is no stain left behind—just like your shirt."

"Why does God care if my heart is clean all of the time?"

"For the same reason you want your shirt to be clean when you go to church," Lemuel answered as she took David's clothes from the washer and put them in the dryer.

"He knows that if your heart is clean you will try to avoid getting it stained in the dirt of sin again. Like you trying to keep your white shirt clean for church. If your heart is already dirty, one more stain won't bother you so much."

"Doesn't God love me regardless of what I do?" David asked.

"Yes, He does love you whether your heart is clean or dirty," Lemuel answered. "So do I, but I still make you go and wash before you eat if you come in the house all dirty from playing outside. If you don't wash and get clean you will eventually get sick from the germs and dirt all over you."

"God knows that the end result of sin is that it hurts us and makes our lives unhappy and ineffective. He wants us to get rid of the destructive effects of sin inside of us as quickly as possible. Just like you wanted to the dirt off of your shirt as soon as Luke got you all dirty."

"I think you're right about that, Grandma," David replied. "I do feel better after I've asked God to forgive me for the bad things I have done. I feel cleaner inside."

"Why do you think you didn't want to wear your dirty clothes to church after Luke jumped up on you?" Lemuel asked.

"I would be embarrassed," David answered. "Everyone would look at me. I would be the only one there in dirty clothes. It wouldn't be comfortable."

"Jesus told a story like that to his disciples once," Lemuel said. "He described a huge wedding reception with the best food you could think of."

"Even better than what you cook?" David asked with a smile.

"Even better than I cook," Lemuel answered. "At this banquet, everyone was given a clean robe to wear. That was Jesus' way of saying that they had all been forgiven and cleansed by God. Just as they were ready to eat, they all saw one man in the back of the room that had tried to come in without a clean robe. Because he did not take the free robe so that he would be clean, Jesus said they tied him up and threw him out of the party."

"Why didn't he want the clean clothes that God had for him?" David asked.

"I'm not sure about that," Lemuel answered. "Maybe he thought he was okay just the way he was. Sometimes people have been dirty for so long that it seems normal to them. They don't even realize that they need to have God forgive them and clean their hearts. Other people are just proud and stubborn and don't want to give up the sin that is in their heart."

"If he didn't want God to make him clean, why did he want to go to God's dinner?" David asked.

"The wedding reception was Jesus' way of describing man's friendship with God. Some people want to have the peace and happiness that comes from knowing God, but they just aren't willing to let go of the bad parts of their lives."

"I'll bet the other people at the party didn't like the dirty guy tracking mud into their party, did they?" David asked.

"Probably not," Lemuel replied. "That's why God wants all of us in the church to keep our lives clean—so that we will be uncomfortable if sin tries to sneak in the door and make everything dirty. You know I don't like it when you track mud into the kitchen after I have just washed the floor."

"I know. You always make me take off my shoes," David replied.

"That's what God wants us to do too," Lemuel said. "If we get dirty with sin, He wants us to take off the dirty clothes and let Him dip them in the waters of forgiveness and rinse them in His cleansing power so that we will be clean enough inside to be uncomfortable if sin comes in again. And if we come to Him with muddy feet from walking around in the sinful world all day, He says to stop and take the dirty shoes off by the door. He spiritually washes our feet, as Jesus did his disciples, so we can be comfortable in His clean house."

"Are my clothes done yet?" David asked. "We'll be late if we don't go pretty soon.

"Here they are, David—just like new. No one will know that you were a mess just a few minutes ago."

"Kind of like the way it is when God forgives us for being bad, huh?" David said with a smile.

"Good answer," Lemuel said. "Once God forgives us, its just like we'd never been dirty at all. He forgets about the dirt and lets us go on with our lives. Speaking of which, let's get going so we won't be late for church."

"I put Luke in the barn so he won't get you dirty again," Esron added.

As David sat in the truck on the way to church, he looked at his white shirt, still warm from the dryer. He remembered what Lemuel said about God washing the spots from his heart when he gets dirty from sin. He liked that image.

As he thought about the story of the wedding reception, he realized that his own heart wasn't as clean as it should be. As they bounced along the road to church, David quietly asked God to spray those spots with the power of His forgiveness and asked Him to rinse his heart to make sure it was clean. It felt good being clean inside.

"Thanks for cleaning my shirt, Grandma," David said. "I feel better now. I hope that when I grow up I can know as much about God as you do. I like the stories you tell me."

"You're welcome, David," Lemuel replied. "If you keep your heart clean and listen to the lessons God teaches you, He will be your best friend. He wants you to get to know Him because He likes you."

"I like Him too," David said. "It feels good to have my heart clean. I'm not embarrassed to talk to God when I know there's no dirty spots in my heart."

APPLYING THE LESSON

Guilt is the pointed finger of self-accusation. Guilt looks at your conduct, feelings and choices and judges them to fall short. Guilt blames you for not being better than you are.

The emotional twin of guilt is shame. Each little cut from the edge of shame's blade goes deeper with every repetition of guilt's ceaseless accusation. As guilt accumulates, shame increases, and the soul begins to pull down the shades of the heart so no one can see the guilt we feel.

> *"Shame is the affect which is the source of many complex and disturbing inner states; depression, alienation, self-doubt, isolating loneliness, paranoid and schizoid phenomena, compulsive disorders, splitting of the self, perfectionism, a deep sense of inferiority, inadequacy or failure, the so-called borderline conditions and disorders of narcissism."*
> John Bradshaw, *Healing the Shame*

In the Christian life, guilt follows sin as the accusing witness. Because we know that God gives us the power to resist sinful behavior, we feel guilt when we fall short. Guilt points a finger at us and declares us not good enough.

When we judge ourselves guilty, we begin to feel shame. And shame drives us into hiding so that others won't see our failures.

Shame is a fear reaction. We fear the rejection of God and others when we feel ashamed. We blame ourselves for doing something wrong and we retreat into hiding to avoid the embarrassment of other people finding out.

Remember how Adam hid in the Garden of Eden after he disobeyed God? He felt guilty and ashamed. He didn't want God to see what he had done. So when he heard God coming, he hid.

Guilt creates a destructive inner conflict. It attacks the self and pushes us to avoid confession, repentance and cleansing. We hide instead. It robs us of the positive power of faith, hope and love—we hide instead of accepting forgiveness.

Learn this: guilt is an act of the will.

It is a secondary response to something we chose to do that we feel was wrong. Although a natural response, it is not the only response that you can choose when you fall short.

For example, on the night Jesus was betrayed, two men sinned. Judas told his enemies where to find him, and three times Peter denied he knew Him. They both did something wrong—they both sinned. Yet each responded to their sin in different ways.

Judas was overwhelmed with guilt, shame and remorse. He chose the ultimate shame-driven retreat into isolation—he committed suicide. Peter wept bitterly, admitted he had failed in that moment and asked God to forgive him—and He did. Peter went on to do great things in his future. Judas is remembered as a traitor and coward. The reason is because they responded differently when they realized they had sinned.

David faced a choice when Luke jumped up and put dirty paw prints all over his good, white shirt. He could blame Luke for being bad; he could internalize his disappointment and embarrassment and decide not to go to church at all that day; or he could go in the house, let Lemuel clean his clothes and go on to church just as clean as when he started the day.

Which of those seems like the healthier choice?

We all see that the mature choice for David is to let Lemuel help him get cleaned up. Yet, when we find that sin has jumped up and stained our hearts, we often let guilt drive us into the arms of shame where we pull back from others and hide our embarrassment.

Remember, everyone sins. You might not see it in others, but we all fall short. The apostle John says that if anyone claims to be without sin, he is not telling the truth.

Then why do we sometimes respond to sin with guilt, shame and embarrassment; why do we pull away and hide so no one will know we failed? I think it is because we forget how easy and healthy it is to just go get cleaned up right away when we fall short.

Guilt and shame do not come from God—they keep you from Him. You create them yourself. They are dysfunctional choices of the will; they actually contradict what God wants to do for you when you fall short—He wants to forgive you and get you cleaned up.

The members of the church in Rome became legalistic and critical of each other because they had set up a set of rules for everyone to follow. If you didn't follow the rules, they criticized you—like eating certain kinds of meat, celebrating certain holy days, etc.

Paul scolds this group, saying "Who are you to judge someone else's servant?" (Romans 14:4). James agrees, adding, "There is only one Lawgiver and Judge, the one is able to save and destroy," (James 4:11).

God does judge us when we do things wrong: He judges us guilty but forgiven.

As Paul says, only God has the right to judge us guilty and condemn us when we fail. He chooses not to. He elects to forgive us instead.

If I condemn myself through guilt or condemn you for falling short, I am trying to take God's job away from Him and be the judge myself. Since you belong to God, I am not authorized to be your judge.

This same principle applies if I decide to use guilt to condemn myself. I become my own judge and find myself guilty. But to do that, I must first kick God out of His job so that I can do the judging for Him.

When I declare myself guilty, I have to push God out of the room and deny that my sin was already paid for and forgiven. He paid the price to forgive all of my sins because He wanted me to be able to spend time at His place without muddy feet. When I choose guilt and shame, I disagree with what God wants.

> *"Therefore, there is now no condemnation for those who are in Christ Jesus . . ."*
> Romans 8:1

Yes, each of us sins. Get over it. That's what forgiveness is for.

Each of us gets mud on our shoes sometimes. Each of us gets paw prints on our shirt. We make bad choices, fall into temptation or say things we shouldn't. Sin is real, and we all fail sometimes—we all fall short and miss the mark, as Paul says.

Because we know that we will sometimes sin, we need to know how to deal with it when it happens. That doesn't mean it's okay or that we accept it. But we know how to get cleaned up when we get dirty.

If we choose guilt and shame instead of forgiveness, it separates us from God and drives us into isolation. Now who would want that? Not God.

The alternative is to confess the sin quickly and allow God to remove the dirty spot through the power of His mercy and forgiveness. Let Him cleanse us with His presence and make us clean and free from guilt or shame.

You cannot choose not to deal with sin. But you can choose how to deal with it when it happens.

Spiritual Exercise

Sin is never good. But it doesn't have to leave a stain.

When I find sin in my heart or behavior, I have a choice to make. Will I internalize my failure with self-accusation and shame, or will I go get it cleaned up right away.

Self-accusation comes with a very high price tag. It punishes your self and separates you from God's will. You choose the path of guilt because you feel you need to be punished. Jesus already took the punishment for that sin and paid the penalty it deserved when He died on the cross—it is called redemption.

Guilt is really a self-destructive form of pride—it says I have right to disagree with God and condemn myself for a sin that He says He has already forgiven. Guilt puts us in conflict with God's will.

Spiritual Exercise, Part I: As you begin to work on this exercise, talk to God about what you are about to do. Tell Him you want to have your heart cleaned and that you want Him to help you identify and remove all destructive guilt from inside yourself. Tell Him that you want to agree with Him about your past sins—that you want to accept that they are forgiven and that you want to feel clean inside again.

After you have prayed, take a piece of paper and write down everything that God brings to your mind that you have ever felt guilty about. Briefly describe your action, attitude and emotions. Describe who was hurt by your behavior and why you think that what you did was wrong.

This is confession. It is admitting your sin and talking to God about it.

Don't rush the process. When you can't think of anything else, stop and ask God to remind you of anything you might have forgotten.

Now look at your list. You have already been forgiven for everything on that list through Jesus. Your next step is to accept God's forgiveness, and that means you have to forgive yourself too—you have to agree with God that those sins are forgiven and that the guilt is gone.

Are you ready to agree with God and let go of your guilt? Cleansing comes when you let go and admit that God is right. When you step into His presence and let Him rinse of any residual dirt that may still be lodged in your heart.

Spiritual Exercise, Part II: Pray through your list one item at a time and specifically release yourself from guilt, self-accusation and self-condemnation.

The Pharisees brought a woman who had sinned to Jesus—she had been caught having sex with someone other than her husband. She was guilty, caught in the act.

So what did Jesus do? He showed her mercy.

First, he turned to the angry mob of people who criticized and condemned her for her failure. He pointed out that each of them had sinned as well—"Let he who has not sinned cast the first stone," He said.

Even though she was guilty, (just like we are at times), Jesus said, *"Neither do I condemn you, go now and leave your life of sin."*

That's exactly what He says to you too. Now can you say that to yourself? Can you choose not to condemn yourself and free your heart to go forward free of the burden of that past sin?

As you read each of the items on your list, listen for Jesus saying, "Neither do I condemn you. . ."

He declares you not guilty and you must do the same thing to yourself if you agree with Him.

> *"Father, I accept your forgiveness of this sin. Thank you for releasing me from guilt. I accept that I am forgiven and that you have declared me 'not guilty.' Today, I agree to accept your release and cleansing from my failure. Help me keep my heart clean from this sin in the future."*

CHAPTER THIRTEEN

THE TRANSFORMATION

---

*"The man on top of the mountain
did not fall there, he
climbed all the way up"*
Vince Lombardi

E very day seemed to surprise David with a new adventure. Today, as he and Lemuel walked back to the house from the pond, he darted into the edge of the woods looking for his next adventure. Lemuel's cancer was slowly sapping her strength and she seemed to walk a little slower every day. But with David's distractions, she always seemed to keep up.

As she walked up to the pasture gate, she noticed David sitting motionless near the brush line.

"Grandma! Come look!" he exclaimed. "There's a big green worm wrapping itself in a blanket," he said.

"That's a caterpillar," Lemuel explained. "It's spinning its cocoon."

"What does it need a cocoon for?" David asked.

"That fat green caterpillar is about to change into a beautiful butterfly. It wraps the cocoon around itself for protection until it is done changing," she added.

"What kind of butterfly will it be?"

"I don't know," Lemuel answered. "We'll just have to wait and see what comes out."

"Do you think it knows it's about to become a new creature that can fly?" David asked.

"I don't know," Lemuel replied. "Do you know what kind of creature God is going to make out of you when He is done?" she asked.

"Of course I do. I'm going to be a man, just like Dad."

"Well, sometimes God has some big changes to make in our lives too. Just like that caterpillar, He can change the person that we are into something new," she added.

"He says we can't even see or imagine what He has planned for us in His Secret Kingdom," she explained.

"Look!" David said. "You can hardly see the caterpillar any more. The cocoon is getting thicker. Can we take it home and see what kind of butterfly comes out?"

"Not today," Lemuel answered. We'll come back and check in a couple of days. Let him finish his work first."

David was so excited about the caterpillar and the cocoon that he insisted that Esron walk out with him to see it after dinner.

"What do you think the caterpillar is thinking right now?" David asked.

"I'd guess it's a little afraid of all of the changes it is feeling all of a sudden," Esron answered. "Yet somehow I think it understands that something beautiful is about to happen even though he can't see it yet."

That night Lemuel read David the Bible story of how God suddenly stopped Saul of Tarsus on his way to Damascus and told him of the new plan He had for his life.

"Remember how the caterpillar built the cocoon to protect itself while it was changing," Lemuel asked. "Why do you think God wants the caterpillar to be alone while it is being transformed?"

"I saw pictures of how caterpillars change," David answered. "It looks yucky. I wouldn't want anybody watching me if I was that kind of mess."

"Did you notice how God did the same thing with Paul after He talked to him that He does with the caterpillar?" Lemuel asked. "After Paul realized who God was and accepted Him, he was sent to a private place to live for three years while God finished changing him,"

"You mean God put him in a cocoon, too?" David laughed.

"Yes, that's right. At some time, God isolates each of us in a private place while we change into the person we are supposed to be."

"Will God put me in a cocoon too?" David asked.

"He already has I think. This summer at the farm is sort of like a cocoon for you. You are away from your friends and all the things you do in the city. It lets you see and learn things you wouldn't see there," Lemuel said. It will happen more than once in your life. One day you will realize you are all alone. You will feel separated from all of the people around you like you are in a cocoon. And there in the quiet of that lonely place, God will come and help you make changes in your life to make you more like Him."

"Sometimes you feel afraid in the dark of the cocoon because you can't see what's coming next," she explained. "But while you are alone, God will transform you into a new creation just lie the butterfly."

"What if I don't want to change?" David asked.

"Well, what if the caterpillar decides it wants to stay a worm

"He can't stay a worm! He was made to become a butterfly."

"Exactly!" Lemuel answered. "And you can't help but change either. Everyone changes. But you only become a butterfly if you change the way God tells you to change."

Every day David would go to the woods and sit and watch the cocoon. It didn't look like anything was happening.

That Saturday Lemuel and David went to check on it together.

"It's sure taking its time!" David said.

"Now that it's done with its cocoon, you can cut the branch off and take it back to the house to watch it," Lemuel said.

"Yes!" David exclaimed. "Can I keep it in my room?"

"Of course," Lemuel answered. "We'll get one of the gallon milk jars and make a new home for the cocoon until it becomes a butterfly."

David poked holes in the lid to let the air get in. He put green leaves and grass in for the butterfly to eat in case it came out when he wasn't watching. He put the jar on the dresser near his bed, so he could watch it every night as he fell asleep and check on it first thing every morning.

About two weeks later, Lemuel was cooking breakfast when she heard David come running down the stairs.

"Grandma, Grandma, Grandma!" he exclaimed. "It's coming out! It's coming out right now! You've got to come and see it!"

"If you are very careful, you can bring the jar downstairs, and we'll all watch it together as it comes out of the cocoon," Lemuel replied.

David sat it right in the middle of the table where they could watch it while they ate breakfast. Slowly the butterfly cut a hole about a quarter of an inch wide in the cocoon.

"The hole's not big enough," David said. "Should I help it make a bigger hole?"

"No, this is something that it has to do by itself," Lemuel replied.

All morning David sat and watched the butterfly and the cocoon. "I think it's stuck," he said. "Nothing's happening."

"Well, maybe it's not in as much of a hurry as you are," Lemuel said with a smile.

As they sat down for lunch, David noticed that the hole was getting a little bigger and the butterfly was trying to pull itself out.

"I still think it's stuck," David said. "I'm going to make the hole a little bigger so it can get out."

"No, you can't do that!" Lemuel answered. "If you try to help the butterfly out of the cocoon, it will never be able to fly by itself. Helping it when it is in the cocoon, actually hurts it."

"But it looks too hard," David said. "It would be a lot easier with a bigger hole. Maybe I should help it just a little."

"If you want the butterfly to be free and be what it is supposed to be, you have to leave it alone," Lemuel said firmly.

"I don't like watching it struggle," David said.

"The struggle makes it strong," Lemuel explained. "Without the struggle, it wouldn't be strong enough to survive outside the cocoon."

"It's hard not to do God's work for Him sometimes," Lemuel said. "We don't like seeing people struggle with problems, but that is often God's way of making them strong and teaching them things."

"You mean God has them in a cocoon too?" David said.

"When we face hard temptations to do something bad, God makes us choose to reject them ourselves. No one can do it for us. He makes a way for us to escape, like the little hole in the cocoon. But we have to pull ourselves out to become stronger."

"Look, Grandma! It's out," David observed. It was a beautiful green Luna moth.

"I think it's resting," David said. "I'll bet it's tired after all that work."

"I'm sure it is," Lemuel said with a smile. "Look, it's starting to eat some of the leaves you put in the jar for it. You can keep it here in the house for a little while, and then we'll go let it go in the pasture where we found it."

"I wish I could be a butterfly too," David said. "It's really pretty."

"You are like the butterfly," Lemuel explained. "God is already changing you into a new person. He's going to make you strong and beautiful just like the butterfly."

"You just have to realize when you're in the cocoon that the changes you are making are turning you into something better," she added.

"A few days ago an old caterpillar went into its cocoon to be transformed," Lemuel explained. "Today, you got to see the beautiful new butterfly that it became. That's a picture of how God uses struggle, pain and the challenges of life to get rid of the old parts of who we are and turn us into something new and beautiful."

Applying The Lesson

Pain hurts. That's why we call it pain. Struggle is always hard. That's what makes it struggle.

Change requires letting go of old things in order to grasp something new. Trials and temptations test the character of every heart. That's why they are the exercises of the soul.

My natural tendency is to avoid pain, struggle and temptation whenever I can. My personal trainer, on the other hand, tells me that, "No pain, no gain; you have to increase the resistance to build your muscle strength; and if you do not choose to overcome the temptation to sit too much, you will become flabby, weak and sick."

God understands the discipline of exercise.

"God disciplines us for our good, that we may share in His holiness. No discipline seems pleasant at the time, but painful. Later on, however, it produces a harvest of righteousness and peace for those who have been trained by it."
Hebrews 12:10, 11

As a teacher, God understands that it is struggle that gives meaning to the lesson. If the task is too easily attained, boredom sets in, and the student loses interest and motivation. Psychologist Viktor Frankl notes that many of his patients come to him complaining of the total and ultimate meaninglessness of their lives.

"They lack the awareness of a meaning worth living for. They are haunted by the experience of their inner emptiness, a void within themselves; they are caught in that situation which I called the 'existential vacuum'"
Viktor Frankl, *Man's Search for Meaning*

The result, he concludes, is boredom. God teaches by experience. It is by experience that God shows us what we are, where we are weak, and how far we walk from the path or righteousness. The reason God reaches us His ways is that it is only by them that we find true inner happiness.

"By wisdom a house is built
and through understanding it is established;
Through knowledge its rooms are filled
with rare and beautiful treasures.

A wise man has great power,
and a man of knowledge increased strength."
Proverbs 24:3-5

David observed the butterfly struggle and fight its way to life. He wanted to help deliver the butterfly from its torment, but he could not. To rescue it from the struggle was to condemn it to a more limited life. It is the same with God in our lives.

Struggle, pain and temptation burden the heart and the mind. We cry for God and others to deliver us from the work of growing in faith and character. But they cannot. Like God, we must wait and watch, for He has designed this very struggle to give us the strength to be free. If you cut the butterfly from the cocoon, it never will have the strength to fly.

But as Solomon said, knowledge fills the rooms of our heart with treasure, strength and power. The knowledge learned from the butterfly is that God allows hardship and discipline because He loves us enough to want to see us transformed from larvae to butterflies.

"For God knew His own before ever they
were, and also ordained that they should be
shaped to the likeness of His Son, that He might
be the eldest among a large family of brothers."
Romans 8:29

King David experienced God's instruction in the school of experience when he was given responsibility to guard and care for his father's flock of sheep, learning the skills of a warrior in protecting the flock from predators like the lion and the bear. If he stayed at home and lived a coddled life, he wouldn't have had the skills or confidence to face Goliath.

After he was anointed to be the next king of Israel, David spent six years fleeing from the armies of Saul who had ordered him killed. It was through this experience that he built his leadership team and learned how to be a leader of other men. After he had grown strong in spirit through many years of struggle, he looked back at how God had instructed him and wrote:

> *"For you, O God, tested us;*
> *you refined us like silver.*
> *You brought us into prison*
> *and laid burdens on our backs.*
> *You let men ride over our heads;*
> *we went through fire and water,*
> *but you brought us to a place of abundance."*
> Psalm 66:10-11

The truth is that you and I determine who we are by the choices we make when faced with struggle, temptation or pain. You have the power to invent and reinvent yourself. Your choices matter to God.

That's why He gives you the power to choose and asks you to choose to follow and love Him—to walk in His ways. He causes us to struggle, to face fear, loss, failure and temptation in order that we may gain the strength that comes from overcoming adversity.

Have you ever seen a slow lazy river? It winds all over the countryside, doesn't it? But find a river flowing rapidly toward its goal and you will find a river running straight and cutting deep. With each obstacle we conquer, we grow stronger, feel more confident and become wiser.

As much as we sometimes wish it were not true, the outcome always comes later. It is all of the choices, actions and responsibilities that precede the outcomes to which we must attend. It is in overcoming the adversities and struggles that we discover life's meaning and deepest joys.

The butterfly cannot concern itself with flying until it has struggled and fought its way out of the cocoon. If it does not have the opportunity to experience that struggle, it will never have the strength to fly. It is the painful struggle against its self-made prison that gives it the strength to fly once it is free.

In some ways, struggle ceases to be struggle and becomes exercise once we realize it is the essential step that leads to a life of freedom. Suffering ceases to be suffering when we find meaning in the purpose of God who brought it to us.

The athlete who goes into strict training rejoices in the struggle experienced by his disciplined regimen, because he knows that this is the path to victory. No one else can run his laps for him, no one can do his weight training, and no one else can eat the healthy diet he needs. Those who love him must, like God, sit back and let him grow strong through the struggle, discipline and pain required to become a great athlete. They do not pity him, however, because they see that what might feel to others as pain and struggle is to the athlete the road to victory and success.

This is the lesson David learned by watching the caterpillar transform into a butterfly and fight its way to freedom from the confines of its cocoon. Suffering, pain and struggle are necessary elements for training the heart, mind and character to be strong in the Lord. It is only through the fire that silver is purified of its dross and only through testing that God makes us strong enough to resist temptation and walk before Him as His children.

As David said, He tests each of His children in order to refine them and ultimately to bring them to the place of abundance.

Don't look for the shortcut to happiness – the road to righteousness runs by the cross.

Spiritual Exercise

It is a paradox that something as distasteful as suffering is uniformly given value by great theologians, philosophers and psychologists of every age.

Why? Because love demands that a child be allowed to experience the struggles necessary to learn right from wrong, weak from strong, and earth from eternity. I imagine it is difficult for the butterfly to understand why it is so hard to get out of the cocoon. I generally don't understand why bad things happen in my life until much later when I am able to look back and see how God has used those experiences to show me His ways and prepare me for what He wants me to do tomorrow.

Spiritual Exercise, Part I:

Briefly describe below the four most difficult experiences you have known in your life. They may be very different and may have been hard for different reasons. Don't try to understand what made them difficult. Just follow your heart and honestly put on paper the hardest struggles you have known. We'll talk more about their significance in a minute.

1. _____

2. _____

3. _____

4. _____

The Danish philosopher Soren Kierkegaard once observed: *"Life must be lived moving forward but it can only be understood looking backward."* I have found this to be how it usually happens in my life. Failure comes, struggle ensues, the money runs out and relationships fail. I sit in the midst of my misfortune and wonder why all of these bad things happen to someone who is a good person, to someone who tries to know God and follow in His ways.

Then after the clouds have cleared and my feet have found the firm footing of the path again, I look back to the struggle I have just come through and see what God has taught me that I never could have seen if He hadn't taken me to the valley and through the dark clouds. I begin to realize how He has strengthened my mind and heart in the fire of tribulation. I thought it was unfair that I should have to endure such trial and indignity, until I saw in the rear-view mirror the loving hand of my personal spiritual trainer giving me the workout that I needed to become a man of character.

> *"Remember how the Lord your God led you all the way in the desert these forty years, to humble you and to test you in order to know what was in your heart, whether or not you would keep His commands. Know then in your heart that as a man disciplines his son, so the Lord your God disciplines you."*
>
> Deuteronomy 8:2

God tested the Israelites to teach them how to overcome their pride and walk humbly before Him and to test their love and obedience toward Him.

Spiritual Exercise, Part II:
For each of the four experiences you have described above, write down your answer to each of the following questions:

1. How did God use this experience to expose my pride and teach me to be more humble?
2. How did this experience help me exercise and gain more character? Did it require me to be patient? Did it demand that I forgive, endure, or learn to be grateful?
3. Was God trying to teach me something about a weakness in my life through this experience? Did my feelings mirror the way I sometimes make God feel because of my own behavior?

4. What did I learn from God's ability to bring me through this type of struggle? Can I trust Him more now that I have survived this experience?
5. What attitudes, behaviors or emotions of mine contributed to the situation that I was required to endure? How can I avoid producing similar problems in the future?

Take the time to do this work. Just reading about exercise doesn't make you stronger.

David learned that the product of struggle was the strength necessary to realize the purpose of the butterfly's creation. Can you identify specific ways in which the struggles you have experienced have made you strong enough to live a Godlier and more successful life? Have the struggles you faced in the past helped prepare you for the challenges you see in the future?

Remember next time God sets you aside and surrounds you in the cloud of adversity that it is here in the cocoon of your personal day of trial that God has come to make you strong enough to fly free in the sunshine of the Spiritual Kingdom.

CHAPTER FOURTEEN

THE SAILOR'S SECRET

---

*"I can't change the direction of the wind,
but I can adjust my sails to
always reach my destination."*
Jimmy Dean

On Saturday morning David found Esron out in the workshop putting together a bookshelf he was building for David's mother. Her birthday was in September, and Esron would give it to her when she came to pick David up in August. David was the carpenter's helper.

David loved the smell of pine boards and sawdust. He put some finishing touches on the big blue birdhouse Esron had helped him build in June, while Esron screwed the brackets onto the shelf. It didn't take David very long to get bored.

"I want to build something else," David said. "What can I make?"

"What do you want to make?" Esron asked.

"I don't know. How about something like an air-plane or a boat?" David answered.

"We can do that," Esron answered. "Let me fin-ish putting these shelves in, and I will help you. You look for a good pine board about two feet long with no knots in it, and we'll start in a minute."

"I want it to be a sailboat so I can use it on the pond," David decided.

Esron showed David how to set the guard on the saw and let him use a push stick to cut the boards for the boat himself. The bottom was made of a three-quarter inch pine board cut four inches wide. The sides were one-quarter inch plywood two inches high. They made the boat sixteen inches long, tapering to a point in the front.

"I hear Lemuel calling us to lunch," Esron said. "We'll have to finish the boat later."

"Can we do it today?" David asked.

"We need to go to town today so that Lemuel can see the doctor," Esron answered. "We'll see if we have time when we get home."

"It sure seems like Grandma has to go to the doctor a lot," David said. "What's wrong with her?"

"Lemuel's been sick for a while," Esron said. "The doctors have to check her out and give her the right medicine to help her keep going."

As they drove to town, David told Lemuel about the boat they were building.

"It's going to be great, Grandma," he explained. "We can go down to the pond and sail together when I'm done."

"Are you a good sailor?" Lemuel asked. "I wouldn't want to get lost at sea."

"Very funny," David said. "It's only the pond. You can't get lost. And besides, I know what I'm doing. After all, I built the boat!"

Before dinner that evening, Esron helped David sand and glue the boat together. Esron wouldn't let David work on Sunday, so it was Monday before David could get back out to paint and finish the board. The made a mast and crossbars from one-quarter inch dowels and Lemuel sewed a sail from some green canvas that had come off of an old lawn chair.

"I want to paint the boat white," David decided.

"I have some white paint here you can use," Esron replied. "Let's put the rudder on first, and then you can get some newspaper and get to painting."

David finished painting the boat about three o'clock that afternoon.

"I'm ready to go sailing," he declared. "Can we go now?"

"No, we have to wait for the paint to dry," Esron answered. "We'll go sail tomorrow after we finish the morning chores."

David brought his boat in and put it right in the middle of the kitchen table during dinner. Esron dug around in the closet and found a handful of old plastic soldiers that had belonged to David's father when he was a boy to put on deck as sailors.

"What are you going to call the boat?" Lemuel asked. "Most boats have names."

"I want to call it 'Wind Catcher,' because it's the best sailboat ever," David said. "When this boat catches the wind, it's going to fly across the water."

David could hardly wait for tomorrow to come so that he could take his boat out for its maiden voyage. Tuesday morning was perfect for sailing. The sky was blue with just a few scattered clouds, and a gentle breeze blew from the west. Lemuel packed a picnic lunch, and they all went down to the pond to sail together.

Lemuel spread out a blanket and sat down with Esron to watch David's regatta.

"Here goes, Grandma," David said as he walked down and put the boat in the water. He gave it a little push, and it floated out just a few feet from the shore.

"Hey, it's not sailing right!" he hollered to Lemuel. "It's just drifting over against the shore."

"Try turning the sail so it catches the wind," Lemuel suggested. "The wind doesn't help if the sail is turned the wrong way."

David turned the sail and tried again. "Look, now it's just going in circles," David complained. "There's something wrong with this boat."

"Maybe the boat is not the problem," Lemuel replied. "Catch the boat and let's try adjusting the sail and rudder again."

"I can't reach it," David said. "I need a stick or something."

"Your boat reminds me of what happens to a lot of people when God tries to show them where to go in their lives," Lemuel observed as they pulled the boat to shore. "God gives them direction, like the wind blowing in the sail of your boat, but unless the sail is set right, they just end up going in circles."

"I don't have a clue what you're talking about," David laughed. "Let's see if we can get the 'Wind Catcher' to sail straight."

So again they adjusted the sail.

"Here we go," David said. "I hope it works this time."

As he pushed the boat out from shore, the wind gusted over the knoll and the boat sailed straight out into the middle of the pond.

"It's working!" David said. "Look at it go! It really goes fast when it works right, doesn't it?"

"Good job," Esron said. "You're really sailing now."

"How are you going to get it back?" Lemuel asked as the boat slowed to a stop in the middle of the pond.

"You'll have to wait for the wind to blow it to the other side of the pond or swim out and get it," Esron observed.

David ran over to the rope swing and swung out into the pond. He spent the next hour until lunch, swimming in the pond with the boat, making adjustment to the sail over and over until it would go where he wanted it to go.

"Look, Grandma," David said. "I can make it go whichever direction I want it to go now, and it will sail back to me in a big circle so that I don't have to swim out and get it. The reason it didn't work at first is that I didn't have the sail set right."

"I can see we've got a real sailor on our hands now," Lemuel replied. "Bring the boat up and let's eat lunch now."

As they ate, Lemuel asked, "Does the wind tell the boat where to go or does the boat tell the wind where to take it?"

"The boat can only go where the wind blows it," David said. "But the wind will not take the boat across the pond unless the sail is set right."

"Good point," Lemuel replied. "That's exactly the way God moves us too. God's direction and guidance flows over us like the wind on your boat, but we only sail in the right direction if we have our hearts set right."

"It's like I have a sail too," David said.

"Just like setting the sail to the right angle determines where your boat will go, so the way you receive God as He moves around you determines where your life will go. You are no different than the sailboat. If the sail in your heart is set right, God will move your life in the right direction. If it is not, you will sail in circles or hit the bank and sit by the shore going nowhere."

"How do I know if my sail is set right?" David asked.

"That sounds like a hard question, but it's not," Lemuel replied. "If you turn your heart straight at God and you let Him have your thoughts, He will lead you straight toward the goals He has for you. If you start to go in the wrong direction, you will start running into walls. When that happens, you know you need to go back and adjust the sails in your heart."

"If I'm like the sailboat, do I have to have a name too?" David asked.

"Maybe we should call you 'Wind Catcher,'" Lemuel said. "If you catch the wind of God's will for you, you will find God sitting right there in the boat with you."

"Cool," David said. "God will go sailing with me. That will be fun."

Lunch was over, so David went back to the pond to sail again. The wind had died down, and the water was a perfect reflection of blue sky and clouds above.

Esron saw the clouds begin to get darker and he was afraid it was going to rain.

"The boat won't go anywhere," David said. "There's no wind."

"Blow on the sail and see if you can make it go on your own," Lemuel suggested.

David blew as hard as he could, but the boat wouldn't move. "I can't blow hard enough," David said. "I need some wind. This isn't working."

"It's that way in our lives too," Lemuel explained. "If we try to make things happen by ourselves instead of finding God's will and letting Him tell us where to go, nothing happens. We huff and puff and blow as hard as we can, but when it is all over and we look back we often see that we really have gotten nowhere at all."

"Let's go back to the house now," Esron interrupted. "It looks like sailing is over for today. I think it's going to rain."

"We'll come back and sail again tomorrow," Lemuel said. "When you get home, put the 'Wind Catcher' where you can see it. Let it remind you to set the sails of your heart to respond to what God tells you to do so that your life will go the right direction."

"It seems like you turn everything we do into a story about God," David joked.

"Everything that happens is a story about God," Lemuel answered. "It happens either because God is trying to show me something or because He wants me to learn how to sail through that event and become a better sailor."

"See what I mean?" David said. "You're doing it again!"

"Just remember to watch for the wind. Check which way it is coming from and set the sails of your heart and mind to follow God. Pretty soon you'll be finding Him in everything that happens to you too."

"Then I'll be a 'Wind Catcher' just like my boat," David said.

"And if you become a 'Wind Catcher,' you will enjoy a voyage through life that will make you happier than any other journey you could take," Lemuel replied.

APPLYING THE LESSON

Once you know that God is a good God—a God of love—then it is reasonable to want His will because you know that He wants the best for you. We cannot love God unless we believe that His intentions for us are good. And we can't accept that His plans are good if we are not willing to accept the direction He wants us to go, even if we do not know the final outcome of the journey.

Hope, the positive expectation of something good, comes before faith. Hope, faith and relationship are the natural bridge that connects God's will to my life in order to turn His will into my will. Without these three powerful tools, the sails of my heart will not be set to accept what God sends my way.

"Do not throw away your confidence; it will be richly rewarded. You need to persevere so that when you have done the will of God, you will receive what He has promised. . . . Now faith is being sure of what we hope for and certain of what we do not see."

Hebrews 10:36; 11:1

Hope expects a positive outcome so it is open God's plan.

Bonnie and Ray came to me thinking of getting a divorce. Conflict had developed in the marriage and they felt like it had been a mistake for them to get married. They just didn't get along. "It was never God's will for us to get married," they declared. "So it can't be wrong for us to get divorced."

Since the Bible tells us most of what God wants us to do, we went there to look for answers. The Bible tells us that God wants married people to stay together except in a few, extreme situations. He hates divorce because of the damage and pain it causes to all of the people involved. Not feeling happy right now was not a good reason for divorce.

It was hard for Bonnie and Ray to believe that God wanted them to stay together because it was not what they wanted right now. "God doesn't want us to be unhappy, does he?" Ray asked.

"God does want you to be happy, Ray," I suggested. "But He wants you to learn to be happy in His will rather than in your own." That's not what Ray and Bonnie wanted to hear.

Bonnie and Ray had lost hope—they did not expect the future to be good for their marriage. Because faith is built on hope (and they didn't have any), they did not have faith to accept that being married was the right choice for them, even though it was what God said He wanted.

The Bible says, "Faith is being sure of what we hope for." It is first expecting good things to happen in the future—hope, and then believing in that future before it arrives—faith. Faith for Bonnie and Ray would have been to believe that if they worked on their relationship and fixed their problems, they could be happy together as a married couple. Because they didn't have hope, they didn't have faith. And without faith, they wanted to give up.

Faith and hope grow in the soil of right relationships—love. When your relationship to God and others is right, you have a positive expectation for the future. That leads to faith and action.

The fact that Bonnie and Ray complained about what God wanted for them, told me that they did not have a right relationship with Him. They did not know Him well enough to know that He was trying to help them and that He knew the best way for them to be happy.

David built a sailboat that was capable of catching the wind and navigating the waters of the pond. In the same way, God has made us capable of knowing and responding to His will. We can be a 'Wind Catcher' if we open the sails of our heart to catch the direction he pushes us as He leads us to the life He designed us to fulfill.

David had to learn that it was not enough to just set the boat in the water. He had to constantly adjust the sails to catch the wind. In our spiritual analogy, we need to adjust our hearts through Bible study and prayer to remain responsive to the direction God is giving us.

If our hearts are turned toward self, if we are set on loving the things in the world, if we are focused on money, power and popularity, our lives will not sail in the right direction when God shows us His will. Bonnie and Ray knew what God's will was; they just didn't like it. They had set the sails of their hearts on feeling good and were headed for a shipwrecked marriage instead of God's will.

Hundreds of books and thousands of sermons have been written on how to find God's will. Usually the focus of these resources is on memorizing the specific content of God's instructions. Now, it is good to know what God wants you to do, but if you do not know God, if your heart is not responsive to His personal direction, you won't end up where He wants you to go.

The first essential step to finding God's will for your life is to get to know Him personally. The better you know someone, the better you understand what they want. When you get to know Him, you will learn that you can trust Him; that He is always on your side. It will make it much easier to respond to His will because you will know that it is what will produces the best outcome in your life.

For ten years, I attended a mega-church with thousands of single adults. Many of these Christians struggle with God's will for them in relationships. They often find that their human desires conflict with what God is telling them. When you look at life from a distance and see the consequences of poor choices, you see that God's way actually protects and guides our lives on a much safer, healthier path.

Those who choose to indulge their own will when it conflicts with God's will end up getting hurt. They experience broken relationships, rejection, emotional injuries and ultimately fill our churches with the walking wounded, because they thought their way was better than God's way. God's way seemed too strict to them, but in the end, it's there to protect them from themselves.

To accept God's will when my human will wants to do something different, I have to be able to see the positive future result of obeying God—that's what hope is. To give up my desire and choose God's will, I have to believe that the outcome of His choice is better than the outcome of my choice--that's faith. In order to have that faith, I need to have a genuine relationship with Him that allows me to trust Him personally.

It took time and patience for David to learn to adjust the sails of his boat to catch the wind and sail in the direction it was intended to go. Learning to walk in God's will also takes time and repeated adjustment in the choices and desires of our hearts.

Sometimes we find ourselves sailing in circles, and we need to adjust the sails. Other times, we may collide with one of God's boundaries, and we need to adjust our direction again.

But the person who patiently makes these adjustments and continues to pursue God's direction, will sail into the positive purpose of God's will for them. It's not always easy to know God's will, but in the end, the reward of finding it is worth the journey.

"The wind blows where it pleases. You hear its sound, but you cannot tell where it comes from or where it is going. So it is with everyone born of the Spirit."

John 3:7, 8.

Spiritual Exercise

The sailor continually monitors the direction and velocity of the wind and adjusts the tack of his sails to maintain course. The same is true of the man or woman who would walk in the center of God's will. The following exercise will help you evaluate adjustments that you may need to make in your heart to correct the direction of your life in relationship to God's will.

Remember that the most important factor in living the will of God is to maintain a close relationship with Him at a personal level—this is the first commandment, to love God.

The foundational source for knowing God's will is the Bible. That's why it is important to read and study it with open ears so we can learn what God has to tell us there.

It is also important to be involved in a good church that teaches and practices what the Bible teaches. This gives you a social support system as you follow God's plan for you. Strong healthy relationships with other Christians make you stronger too.

Spiritual Exercise, Part I: The following exercise will help you check on your sails and determine in what direction God is leading you. As you work through this exercise, be a 'Wind Catcher.'

1.   What one thing could I start or stop doing right now that would most change my relationship with God?

_____

How would making this change alter my life's direction?

_____

2.   Of all the things God has asked me to do or not to do, what is the hardest for me?

_____

What makes it so hard to accept of God's will for me?

_____

3.   Specifically describe three areas where your desires conflict with what God wants you to do.

_____
_____
_____

What do you think makes you want these things that conflict with what God wants?

_____

4.   What things have happened in your life that are hard to be grateful about?

_____

Why is it hard to believe these things were part of God's plan for you?

_____

Spiritual Exercise, Part II: The life of King David provides a useful study in the benefits and costs associated with choosing to obey or reject God's will. There were many times when David chose to follow the wind of God's direction at great risk to himself. He discovered that God's path always took him to a better place eventually.

There were other times, however, when David specifically disregarded God's guidance and exercised his own contradictory choices. That's when he discovered the tremendous cost and pain of ignoring the direction of the wind. He ended up shipwrecked.

Beginning in the book of I Samuel, Chapter 16, study the life of David and take careful notes on when he chose to follow God's guidance and when he chose to go his own way. Observe the outcome of these contrasting choices. By studying the example of how God led and directed the life of David, your own faith, hope and love for God will grow.

To know and follow God's will requires familiarity with the Bible; the fellowship of other Christians and a close relationship with God. It requires active listening to His voice as He speaks to you though the Bible, in prayer and through other people.

It also requires hope—a positive expectation of the future good He has for you and faith—the belief that the future He has planned for you is both real and good. But as you study God's will, always remember that His greatest wish for you is love—a right relationship with Himself.

CHAPTER FIFTEEN

WHY BIRDS STOP SINGING

"They shall all be taught by God."
Jesus

Each morning Lemuel quietly escaped from the noise and clatter of the kitchen to read and pray on the sanctuary of her back porch. At one end of the porch hung a white porch-swing built for two. Along the wall under the kitchen window were two black cane rockers with a small wicker table between them. There, in the shadow of the hardwood grove and in view of the orchard, Lemuel talked to God.

A birdbath sat twenty feet out from the back steps, and a bird feeder Esron had built hung nearby. Here she watched the birds come and go; die and grow; sing and raise their young. Her quiet sanctuary thundered with ever changing activity each morning.

Twice a week David mixed sugar and red dye with two cups of water to fill the hummingbird feeder that hung from the edge of the eaves. Whenever birdseed in the feeder ran low, Esron would take the bird feeder down from its pole, where it hung beyond the reach of the ever-hungry squirrels, and have David fill it with fresh birdseed.

David filled the feeders this Saturday morning and was sitting with Lemuel on the porch watching the birds enjoy their fresh breakfast, while a squirrel tried to figure out how to get down to the bird feeder and steal some free lunch for himself.

"How come the squirrels never stop trying to get the birdseed?" David asked. "They should know by now it's not for them."

"They see it, want it; and don't think about anything else," Lemuel replied.

A small red hummingbird darted up to sample the fresh nectar David had prepared for it. David sat very still so that he would not scare it away. He watched it hang in midair in front of them as if suspended by a magic thread.

"How can it just hang there without flying anywhere?" David asked. "I thought birds used the airflow over their wings like an airplane to create the lift they need to stay up."

"Every creature is different," Lemuel replied. "You can learn something from each thing God has made. There is a little secret about God hidden in each of His creations."

"Look, Grandma, the birds are fighting again," David said, pointing to the birdbath. "It seems like the blackbirds are always mad at the sparrows."

"They just won't leave them alone, will they?" Lemuel replied. "I guess they think that because they are bigger and stronger, the birdbath belongs to them."

"Look, there's an oriole at the feeder," David said. "Why did God make so many different kinds of birds? I can't keep track of them all."

"I'm not sure," Lemuel answered. "Once He started making them, I think He liked it so much He just couldn't stop."

"Listen, what kind of bird is that?" David asked when he heard the call of a warbler in the old maple tree."

"I don't hear it," Lemuel answered. "Was a bird singing? My old ears don't hear as much as they used to when I was your age," she added. "Why, just last summer I was sitting right here reading and watching the birds, when I suddenly realized that the birds didn't sing anymore."

"Why didn't they sing, Grandma," David asked.

"That's what I wanted to know too," she answered. "But then I looked closer and noticed a meadowlark in the plum tree, right over there. I could see its throat moving and its beak would open and close—I could see that it was singing, but I couldn't hear a sound."

"What was wrong with it?" David asked.

"Nothing was wrong with it," Lemuel replied. "I realized that the birds were still singing, I just couldn't hear them anymore."

"What did you do?" David asked. "Did you feel sad that you couldn't hear the birds sing?"

"I did feel sad. I felt like I had lost something important," she answered. "I just sat there for a long time watching the birds; wishing I could hear them sing.

"But I realized that I could still hear something much more important—I could still hear God's voice when He talked to me. Many people don't know that God speaks all around us, like the sound of the birds when we sit on the back porch."

"Why do they think God doesn't speak any more?" David asked.

"Because they can't hear Him they don't think He is speaking," she answered. "At first I thought the birds didn't sing any more. It took me a minute to realize that the birds were still singing but I wasn't hearing them any more. I had to go to town the next week and get a hearing aid to put in my ear so I could hear better again.

"A lot of people are like I was with the birds; they can't hear God speaking, so they think He's not talking to them at all."

"What God says is important," David added. "Why would people stop listening to what He says?"

"Sometimes I think they just get too busy and forget to listen," Lemuel answered. "Other times they walk too far away from God and can't hear Him any more. They want to go their own way and they don't want God telling them what they should do."

"I like listening to what God says when I am reading the Bible, or listening to one of your stories," David said. "I hope I don't forget to listen to His voice."

"Just like the birds keep singing, God will always speak," Lemuel said. "Because He wants to help you and be your friend, He will always have something to say to help you. But, you have to be quiet enough inside to hear His voice over everything else that's going on—just like listening to the birds sing."

"Sometimes I'm not sure if God is saying something, or if I am just talking to myself," David said. "How can I tell if it is really God talking to me?"

"Remember how at the beginning of the summer, you said all of the birds sounded alike?" Lemuel asked. Now you have learned the difference between the sound of he whippoorwill, the warbler and the chickadee. How did you learn to tell the difference between the songs of the different kind of birds?"

"Well, I listened to them for a long time, and then I could tell that they made different sounds when they sang. I could tell the difference between each of them when I heard them sing," David answered.

"That's exactly how you learn to hear God's voice too," Lemuel said. "If you want to know God's voice, you have to concentrate and listen for it. When you read the Bible, ask Him to talk to you about what it means as you read. When you think He has told you something, see if agrees with what He told other people in the Bible. That's how you learn to tell the difference between God's voice and your voice."

"What if I can't hear God's voice when I want to?" David asked. "What do I do then?"

"Last summer, when I realized I couldn't hear the birds, I had to go to the ear doctor and get my ear examined. He gave me the hearing aid, so I could hear the birds again," Lemuel explained.

"That's what you need to do too. If you can't hear what God is saying, examine your heart to see if there is too much other stuff in the way, blocking the sound of what God is saying."

"Sometimes, even when I listen hard, I can't hear Him very well," David said.

"Sometimes you need to get a hearing aid like I did for my ear. If you check your heart and everything is right with God and you still can't hear, ask Him to help you through His living Spirit that He has sent to be in your heart. Like that little brown hearing aid in my ear, He will amplify what God is saying so you can hear it better."

"You mean I need a hearing aid too?"

"We all need some help hearing what God has to say sometimes," Lemuel explained. "It's easy to get distracted by things that we have to do or want to do. The Spirit in us keeps calling us back to God like the song of the birds in the plumb tree tries to get your attention every morning."

"What happens if I stop listening?"

"You would lose something beautiful from your life," Lemuel explained. "Just like me when I couldn't hear the birds any more. You would lose the feeling of friendship and direction that comes from talking to God each day as your best friend."

"Well, I don't want to lose that," David declared.

"It is a lot to lose," Lemuel answered. "Jesus once asked the religious people, who did not want to listen to what he had to say, what good it would do them if they succeeded at everything in life but lost their own souls."

"They'd have a lot of stuff but they wouldn't be able to enjoy it," David answered.

"Good answer," Lemuel replied. "If your friendship with God is strong and you listen to His voice, you will be able to enjoy everything He gives you. If you don't, you won't.

"Some people work hard to make money and succeed, but if they don't have a friendship with God, they miss the happiness that comes from living in the Spiritual Kingdom. They have a lot of stuff, but no way to enjoy it."

"I'd rather have less stuff and enjoy it more," David said.

"If you walk beside God and listen to His voice, you will have a happier life than the people with all the stuff," Lemuel answered. "If you listen to His voice, you will know what it is to have a friend who is always there, someone who cares about everything that happens to you. That's the thing that has made my life so happy."

"I want to be happy like you when I get old."
"Keep walking in the Spiritual Kingdom and you will be. Listen carefully each day for God's voice, like we sit and listen to the birds on the porch in the morning. See what direction He is going that day, like the wind guiding your sailboat, and let Him show you where to go. He will be your best friend. I've lived eighty years in the Spiritual Kingdom, and I wouldn't want to live anywhere else."

"Whenever I hear the birds sing, I'm going to stop and listen for what God has to say too," David decided. "I want to know what He is up to, so I can do it too."

"I'm glad you told me about the Spiritual Kingdom, Grandma," David said as he gave her a hug. He wasn't sure why there was a tear coming down Lemuel's cheek as she held him tight for a long time that morning. But he knew everything was going to be okay.

APPLYING THE LESSON

Spiritual deafness is the deadliest disease of the human heart.

Its victims slowly grow cold and die a spiritual death, which separates them from the purpose and source of life. Because it separates them from God, it separates them from the future He has planned for them.

The story Lemuel told actually happened to me when I recently went to visit my own elderly father in Minnesota. He talked about the garden where he loved to spend his days and then said, "I wondered why the birds didn't sing any more, until I saw a little bird singing at the edge of the garden. I could see its throat move, but I couldn't hear it. Then I knew that the birds were still singing but that I had stopped hearing them."

I tried to swallow the lump in my throat as I considered the impact of the aging process on my own father. As I drove home I thought, "How much sadder it is for those who have stopped hearing God's voice when He speaks to us in the Spiritual Kingdom."

Nothing could be more meaningless than to realize when I am old, that I have lived a successful life in all of the ways that do not matter but missed the one thing that actually makes a difference—the life of my own soul. It is a tragedy to realize at the end of life that it was lived without meaning; without the breeze of God's direction at our backs to guide us forward; without the power of His love to give to others to make their lives meaningful and happy—lives with purpose and direction.

How sad to build a life full of treasures only to realize in the end that I must walk into eternity with empty hands *and* an empty heart.

Jesus was clear about the consequences of spiritual deafness—of the result produced by a life lived outside of a genuine relationship with God.

"Remain in me, and I will remain in you. No branch can bear fruit by itself; it must remain in the vine. Neither can you bear fruit unless you remain in me.

"I am the vine, you are the branches. If a man remains in me and I in him, he will bear much fruit; apart from me you can do nothing. If anyone does not remain in me, he is like a branch that is thrown away and withers; such branches are picked up, thrown into the fire and burned."

John 15:4-6

Spiritual deafness separates us from God—from the vine. The result is that He can't produce life through us. The people of Jesus' day had a deadly spiritual disease—they couldn't hear God's voice, but they claimed to be experts in what He wanted anyway. They were faking it. They worked hard at their religion but it was all man-made—God wasn't a part of it. When God came to them in the living form of His Son, they killed Him to shut Him up. They were so committed to their fake religion that they refused to listen to anything God wanted to say to them.

They were experts in what the written instructions were. They added thousands of rules of their own.

But they were spiritually deaf. They could not hear the voice of God in their hearts.

> *"You have never heard His voice nor seen his form, nor does His word dwell in you, for you do not believe the one he sent. You diligently study the Scriptures because you think that by them you possess eternal life. These are the Scriptures that testify about me, yet you refuse to come to me to have life."*
>
> John 5:37-40

A short time later, Jesus again said how important it was to listen to God.

> *"It is written in the prophets: 'They will all be taught by God.' Everyone who listens to the Father and learns from Him comes to me."*
>
> John 6:45

The same disease is prevalent in modern culture just as it was when Jesus walked the roads of Galilee. For example, you don't have to go too far to hear preachers and writers tell people to follow the desire of their own heart, as an indicator of what God wants for them. They start telling God what He should give them instead of listening for what He wants. "Surely God wouldn't give me this desire if He didn't want me to have it."

Yet when we read the Bible, we read that God actually wants the opposite result—that we die to the desires of our own hearts and learn to live by the desires of His heart.

"The cravings of sinful man, the lust of his eyes and the boasting of what he has and does — comes not from the Father but from the world. The world and its desires pass away, but he man who does the will of God lives forever."

I John 3:16, 17

Like the Leaning Tower of Pisa, the human heart naturally leans away from God. It naturally seeks its own pleasure over what is best in the long run. It is only when the heart learns to hear the voice of God that it is led to a different path of eternal wisdom—a path that leads to a life of purpose, meaning and service to others.

"Those who live according to the sinful nature have their minds set on what that nature desires; but those who live in accordance with the Spirit have their minds set on what the Spirit desires. The mind of sinful man is death, but the mind controlled by the Spirit is life and peace; the sinful mind is hostile to God. It does not submit to God's law, nor can it do so. Those controlled by the sinful nature cannot please God."

Romans 8:5-8

Paul taught his students the importance of replacing the inner voice of man with the Spiritual voice of God. He hammered home the importance of replacing our ways with God's ways. He taught that maturity could only be reached by listening to God's voice rather than the voice of my selfish desires.

"So I tell you this, and insist on it in the Lord, that you must no longer live as the Gentiles do, in the futility of their thinking . . . You were taught, with regard to your former way of life, to put off the old self, which is being corrupted by its deceitful desires; to be made new in the attitude of your minds, and to put on the new self, created to be like God in true righteousness and holiness."

Ephesians 4:17, 22-24

God's voice will usually lead us away from the natural desires of the heart. That's why the Christian life sometimes feels like sacrifice. Paul called it dying to the old self. Jesus struggled in the Garden of Gethsemane between the human desire to save his life and God's desire to have him become the living sacrifice for sin. He had to make a choice. He chose to listen to God and walk on the path prepared for Him.

Jesus told a story of ten virgins waiting for a wedding—a picture of the church. All ten fell asleep, but five were wise and five were foolish. The five wise virgins had filled their hearts with the oil of God's presence so that they were prepared. The foolish virgins had hearts that were empty. When the day came suddenly, the wise virgins were ready and the others lost out.

Even though Lemuel lost her hearing, she was smart enough to go get the help she needed—a hearing aid. When the voice of God grows dim, we must do what the wise virgins in Jesus' story did; we must fill our hearts with the oil of God's presence so we can hear his voice again.

We have had many adventures on our journey with Lemuel and David into the Spiritual Kingdom, but they all end up in the same place. They all lead to God Himself, to the place where His voice can be heard, His direction seen and His love felt in our hearts. Come walk with Lemuel in the Spiritual Kingdom and listen to the music of God's voice as He speaks to you. Set the sails of your heart to respond to His direction and, at the end of the day, find peace and purpose in the life you were intended to live.

Spiritual Exercise

It is easy to sit on the back porch of life, settle into the rocker and fall asleep. Then, when you suddenly wake up, you realize that the voice of God has gone silent around you. The birds have stopped singing. The only voice you hear is your own.

In this exercise, we will work to improve our listening skills. Listening to God's voice and discerning His ways is the only method of keeping our feet secure on the narrow path that leads to God.

Spiritual Exercise, Part I: When King David realized that he had wandered off and could not hear God's voice, he wrote a Psalm to tell God how hungry he was to taste His presence once again.

Go to Psalm 42 in your Bible and read it three times without stopping. Picture David as he prayed this prayer; feel his emotion. Consider why it was so serious to him that he couldn't hear what God had to say.

Now, pray the Psalm slowly, one line at a time as your prayer, asking God to come close and speak to you in your heart so you can hear His voice.

Spiritual Exercise, Part II:

After you have finished praying Psalm 42, take a piece of paper and write a letter to God expressing your personal desire to hear His voice. Like the song of the birds in Lemuel's backyard, express your own desire to be able to differentiate between the voice of self and the voice of God's Spirit in you. Like Lemuel's hearing aid, ask God to amplify His voice so you can hear it.

Finally, as you read the Bible each day for the next week, read just a few verses and then stop; clear your mind of analysis and questions; ask God to put in your mind what He wants to say to you through that passage of Scripture.

Listen quietly for the voice of His Spirit in you.

Good listening skills are learned through practice—practice every day.

> *"No discipline seems pleasant at the time, but painful. Later on, however, it produces a harvest of righteousness and peace for those who have been trained by it."*
>
> Hebrews 12:11

Go back and complete the spiritual exercises in this book every year until the process of growing strong and mature in your walk with God is complete; until it becomes natural for you to turn and listen to God's voice in the mist of each of life's activities.

Become a listener and you will soon become a follower.

We have taken a journey into the Spiritual Kingdom with Lemuel and David. Don't stop walking just because the book is done. Like Lemuel, look for the ways God shows himself in the world around you every day, sometimes right in your own backyard. Follow the sound of the voice you hear and stay close to Him.

Jesus called himself a good shepherd. He calls His own sheep personally, by name and they follow Him because they know the sound of His voice.

The two key traits of those who live in the Spiritual Kingdom are these: They hear and then they follow.

God wants you to live your life close to Him.

Do you agree?